DATE DUE

Steve
Jobs

The People to Know Series

Madeleine Albright
0-7660-1143-7

Neil Armstrong
0-89490-828-6

Isaac Asimov
0-7660-1031-7

Robert Ballard
0-7660-1147-X

Barbara Bush
0-89490-350-0

Willa Cather
0-89490-980-0

Bill Clinton
0-89490-437-X

Hillary Rodham Clinton
0-89490-583-X

Bill Cosby
0-89490-548-1

Walt Disney
0-89490-694-1

Bob Dole
0-89490-825-1

Marian Wright Edelman
0-89490-623-2

Bill Gates
0-89490-824-3

Ruth Bader Ginsberg
0-89490-621-6

John Glenn
0-7660-1532-7

Jane Goodall
0-89490-827-8

Al Gore
0-7660-1232-8

Tipper Gore
0-7660-1142-9

Billy Graham
0-7660-1533-5

Alex Haley
0-89490-573-2

Tom Hanks
0-7660-1436-3

Ernest Hemingway
0-89490-979-7

Ron Howard
0-89490-981-9

Steve Jobs
0-7660-1536-X

Helen Keller
0-7660-1530-0

John F. Kennedy
0-89490-693-3

Stephen King
0-7660-1233-6

John Lennon
0-89490-702-6

Maya Lin
0-89490-499-X

Jack London
0-7660-1144-5

Malcolm X
0-89490-435-3

Wilma Mankiller
0-89490-498-1

Branford Marsalis
0-89490-495-7

Anne McCaffrey
0-7660-1151-8

Barbara McClintock
0-89490-983-5

Rosie O'Donnell
0-7660-1148-8

Gary Paulsen
0-7660-1146-1

Christopher Reeve
0-7660-1149-6

Ann Richards
0-89490-497-3

Sally Ride
0-89490-829-4

Will Rogers
0-89490-695-X

Franklin D. Roosevelt
0-89490-696-8

Steven Spielberg
0-89490-697-6

John Steinbeck
0-7660-1150-X

Martha Stewart
0-89490-984-3

Amy Tan
0-89490-699-2

Alice Walker
0-89490-620-8

Andy Warhol
0-7660-1531-9

Simon Wiesenthal
0-89490-830-8

Elie Wiesel
0-89490-428-0

Frank Lloyd Wright
0-7660-1032-5

People to Know

Steve Jobs

Wizard of Apple Computer

Suzan Wilson

Enslow Publishers, Inc.

40 Industrial Road   PO Box 38
Box 398   Aldershot
Berkeley Heights, NJ 07922   Hants GU12 6BP
USA   UK

http://www.enslow.com

To Brett and Reed,
Computer Wizards of the future

Library of Congress Cataloging-in-Publication Data

Wilson, Suzan.
    Steve Jobs : wizard of Apple computers / Suzan Wilson.
        p. cm. — (People to know)
    Includes bibliographical references and index.
    ISBN 0-7660-1536-X
    1. Jobs, Steven, 1955– 2. Businesspeople—United States—Biography. 3. Apple
Computer, Inc. 4. Computer industry—United States. I. Title. II. Series.
    HD9696.2.U62 J63   2001
    338.7'6100416'092--dc21   2001001611

Printed in the United States of America

10 9 8 7 6 5 4 3 2 1

To Our Readers
We have done our best to make sure all Internet addresses in this book were active and appropriate when we went to press. However, the author and the publisher have no control over and assume no liability for the material available on those Internet sites or on other Web sites they may link to. Any comments or suggestions can be sent by e-mail to comments@enslow.com or to the address on the back cover.

Every effort has been made to locate all copyright holders of material used in this book. If any errors or omissions have occurred, corrections will be made in future editions of this book.

Illustration Credits: © Corel Corporation, pp. 15, 42, 44, 48; Angie Lemus-Groseclose, Encinitas, California, p. 83; Apple Computer, Inc., pp. 110, 112 (insets); Associated Press, pp. 6, 36; ClassMates.Com Yearbook Archives, p. 28; Courtesy of <http://www.pcbiography.net>, p. 81; Courtesy of NeXT Software, Inc., p. 100; Diana Walker/Getty Images, pp. 64, 73, 78, 89, 94; Enslow Publishers, Inc., p. 103; Gary Parker/Getty Images, p. 55; Moshe Brakha/Getty Images, p. 107; Photo by Dan Weinberg, p. 23; Pixar Animation Studios, p. 112 (product insets, Apple Computer, Inc.); Private collection, pp. 39, 61, 69, 76; Unisys Corporation, p. 18; Used with permission from Glen Sanford, <http://www.apple-history.com>, p. 11.

Cover Illustration: Bob Riha/Getty Images

Contents

Steve Jobs in 1977.

Mission Nearly Impossible

Twenty-one-year-old Steve Jobs stepped out of the Byte Shop in Mountain View, California, with an order for fifty Apple computers. It was more than even he had hoped for—because the computers he had just sold did not yet exist.[1]

It was April 1976, and Jobs looked like many young men of the 1970s, dressed in jeans, T-shirt, and sandals (when he wore shoes) and adorned with long dark hair and beard. He rushed to a telephone to tell his partner that they had thirty days to manufacture and deliver the order. Jobs had no doubt that they could meet the challenge, but first he had to talk someone into giving them what they needed: that is, $20,000 to buy parts.

His partner, Steve Wozniak, was flabbergasted.

What had Jobs gotten them into? They had planned to sell printed circuit boards for computers, not fully assembled computers.[2] The company, which they called Apple, had very little money and no place to assemble its product. Also, many details about the design and operation still had to be worked out. It would be a difficult if not impossible thirty-day task.

After one banker refused the company a loan, Steve Jobs realized that because of his appearance, no banker was likely to take him seriously. Also, the two young men had no experience in business, and the computer they were manufacturing had no sales record.

Jobs tried to talk an electronics supplier into giving him parts in exchange for a share of the Apple company. The offer was declined because the supplier, like many others, thought Apple had no future and did not want to own part of a company that would fail.[3]

Until the seventies, when the microprocessor was invented, computers were room-sized machines that businesses used to keep records and do complicated calculations. Even hobbyists never imagined that small, desktop computers would ever be available to all people. But Steve Jobs was not a hobbyist; he was a visionary. He had already predicted that every home would eventually have a computer.[4] And he was willing to work endless hours and talk to countless people to stay at the front of this technological movement.

Jobs managed to borrow $5,000 from a friend, and then found a company in Palo Alto that was willing to sell him $15,000 worth of components on thirty days' credit.[5] That meant that Apple could get the parts and assemble the fifty computers without paying any money. Within thirty days, however, Jobs would have to pay up. He would have to deliver the finished computers and collect money from the Byte Shop to pay for the electronics. Apple Computer Company was in business.

Once Jobs had the electronics, Apple needed a place to assemble the computers. Up until then, all work had been done in Jobs's bedroom, but the operation had outgrown that. Components for fifty computers took up a lot of space, so Jobs expanded down the hall to his married sister Patty's old room. The dresser drawers were heavy with small parts like transistors and capacitors. Boxes stacked in corners bulged with circuit boards. The bed was the only place to sit, though it was covered with computer parts. Within weeks, the Apple operation had taken over the garage as well.

Apple needed help with its first assembly line, so Jobs hired Patty and a couple of high school boys to insert various electronic components into numbered holes on printed circuit boards. Then everything was soldered into place. Assembly took about six hours for each computer. The soldering gun left scorch marks on Jobs's desk, and occasionally, parts were plugged in the wrong way, causing defective machines.[6]

When Jobs delivered the first dozen computers to the Byte Shop, the owner was somewhat confused. What he saw were partial computers, not the fully assembled computers he had expected. Where were the peripherals: the keyboard, television, power supply, and case? Jobs argued that what Apple had manufactured were fully assembled printed circuit boards—the heart of the computer— and buyers or the Byte Shops could easily add the peripherals. The owner honored his agreement and paid for the computer boards. Jobs left the Byte Shop with $6,000.

After talking to the Byte Shop owner, Jobs decided that he would provide wooden cases and help the shops order the parts necessary to turn the Apple I circuit boards into full computers.[7] In addition, he agreed that Wozniak, the computer's designer, would find a way to load BASIC—a computer programming language—into the computer's memory. This meant that Apple had even more work to do, but no extension of delivery date.

Steve Jobs knew that to be successful, Apple Computer Company had to give the appearance of an established business, not a do-it-yourself operation. He had already dealt with many people who had no confidence in the company, and he wanted to appear professional. Rather than use his home address, he rented a post office box in Palo Alto. Then he arranged for Apple's business calls to be routed to an answering service. Jobs got the messages and returned the calls. He also bought advertisements in two magazines. Outsiders were given the impression that Apple Computer Company was a serious business.

Wozniak had a full-time job working for Hewlett-Packard, but he and Jobs sometimes worked through the night to fix bugs in their system or repair any

The Apple I was just a printed circuit board—the heart of the computer. Jobs, right, and Woz display their 1976 creation.

defectively assembled circuit boards. Jobs wrote an owner's manual, delivered orders, and constantly shopped for better deals. When he was not at Jobs's house, Wozniak worked at home writing programs and continually upgrading his version of the BASIC program. Every few days, Jobs hand delivered updated copies to every Byte Shop that sold the Apple I. As money came in from selling the first fifty computers, it went right back into the company to upgrade components or improve operations.

The twenty-ninth day after he had made the agreement, Steve Jobs walked into the Byte Shop with the last of the fifty computers. The next day he handed the electronics distributor payment for all the parts. The challenge had been met just as Steve Jobs predicted. Apple Computer had sold fifty computers to retail shops. Apple employees immediately started work on the next fifty.

In 1976, an apple was simply a fruit. People grew apples, ate apples, and played games like bobbing for apples. Before the end of that year, *Apple* had taken on an entirely different meaning. People now manufactured Apples, programmed Apples, and played games on Apples. Within six years, Apple Computer would be known as the fastest-growing company in America.

Steve Jobs would talk to many people about various aspects of business and computers on his way to becoming an influential but controversial corporate leader. Jobs had ideas. He had the personality and motivation to turn those ideas into salable products. How could he do this? Simple. All his life, Steve Jobs liked to think different.

Brilliance
by Bribery

Steven Paul Jobs was born on February 24, 1955, in San Francisco, California. A few weeks later he was welcomed into the lives of his adoptive parents, Paul and Clara Jobs.

Steve's parents had met soon after the end of World War II. Paul Jobs was stationed on a U.S. Coast Guard ship that was being decommissioned in San Francisco. He bet a shipmate that he could find a wife in this city by the Golden Gate Bridge. He won the bet. He and Clara met on a blind date, and they married in 1946.

Paul Jobs had grown up in the Midwest and had dropped out of high school to join the U.S. Coast Guard. He became a skilled machinist, tending and repairing ships' engines. When Clara met the six-foot-tall guardsman in San Francisco, Paul had short hair and several tattoos. Clara Jobs, a good-natured accountant, moved to the Midwest with her new husband.

For six years Paul Jobs worked as a machinist for International Harvester and as a used-car salesman. Then, in 1952, he and Clara moved back to San Francisco. Three years later they adopted a son, Steven Paul, and bought a house in South San Francisco.

Steve was a bright, active child who learned early to get his own way. He just cried until his parents did what he wanted. When he was two years old, baby Patty joined the family, and Steve had to share the world with his adopted sister.

Even as a toddler Steve showed a willingness to experiment, to take risks. His first experiment with electricity was to jam a metal bobby pin into an electric outlet. The electric current not only shocked him, it burned his hand and he ended up in the hospital for treatment. A year later he and a friend experimented with bottles of ant poison. They drank their experiment and were rushed to the hospital to get their stomachs pumped—a great discomfort to the boys, though they suffered no lasting effects.

Steve never required much sleep. His normal waking time was four in the morning. His sleep-deprived parents finally bought him a rocking horse, a record player, and some records so that he could amuse himself and they could sleep.

Steve's father loved cars. Paul Jobs bought, fixed, and resold them. His tidy garage was full of car parts that he always bargained for. His son was usually

Steve spent his early childhood years in San Francisco, home of the Golden Gate Bridge.

with him on buying trips, so Steve started learning the language of negotiations and bargaining before he started school.

In 1961, when Steve was six, the family moved to nearby Mountain View. Clara Jobs worked at a bowling alley during the day and baby-sat at night to pay for her children's swimming lessons. Steve joined the Mountain View Dolphins Swim Club, but he never seemed to fit in. He liked competition, but only if he won. When he lost a race, he would go off by himself and cry. Other boys would taunt him and snap him with wet towels. Steve was never one of the guys.[1]

Steve had learned to read before kindergarten, and he was often bored in school. But being unusually inquisitive and daring, he could not just sit still. He was a class cutup and refused to do anything he felt was a waste of time. In third grade he and some friends let snakes loose in the classroom and exploded bombs. They were expelled from school. He said in a later interview, "We basically destroyed our teacher."[2]

Steve was sensitive to things happening around him, and when his fourth-grade teacher asked, "What is it in this universe that you don't understand?" he answered, "I don't understand why all of a sudden we're so broke."[3] Until recently his father had provided adequately for the family, but now the family no longer took vacations or bought new things. Steve was perplexed.

More than a year earlier, Paul Jobs's friend had talked him into becoming a real estate salesman. Many homes were being built and sold in the valley near San Francisco (later known as Silicon Valley), but Paul Jobs did not like selling real estate. He went back to what he did best—being a machinist. He had to start at the bottom of the pay scale and work his way up. So for a couple years, even though Clara Jobs had a part-time job, the family had financial problems.

Many of the men in the neighborhood worked in the electronics industry. An engineer from Hewlett-Packard, who lived a few doors down from the Jobses, brought a microphone home one day. Steve was intrigued with it and badgered the neighbor until he told Steve the secret of the device. The engineer was delighted to share his knowledge with Steve and invited him to dinner to talk about electronics.

He also invited ten-year-old Steve to join the Explorer Club, an organization sponsored by Hewlett-Packard for children interested in engineering. Company engineers demonstrated the latest products, such as room-sized business computers, calculators, and lasers. After a meeting about holograms, Steve talked his way into a tour of the lab. The engineers showed Steve how lasers were used to make three-dimensional pictures on sheets of photographic paper. They were impressed with Steve's intensity and seriousness and gave him an old hologram etched on glass. It became one of his most prized possessions.[4]

Steve liked to show off his electronic gadgets and knowledge to the neighborhood kids. One boy, Jeff Eastwood, reported that half the time they did not know what he was talking about. Steve would show

*Early computers, like the ENIAC, designed by J. Presper Eckert, Jr.,
above, filled a whole room. Ten-year-old Steve joined the Explorer
Club to learn about new technology.*

them things that no one could understand. Jeff would go home and say to his dad, "He's lying again."[5]

Usually, all the children in Steve's neighborhood played together. A favorite activity was making movies. One of the kids had a Super-8 movie camera and filmed stories his friends acted out. Steve's favorite role was putting on his father's raincoat and hat and playing a detective or a spy.

Steve finally found a friend in his fourth-grade teacher, Imogene Hill. She seemed to understand him. She recognized that he was unusually bright even though his work did not show it. She bribed him with money to produce good-quality schoolwork. For example, when he finished a workbook she would give him $5. From her, Steve developed a love of learning and a fondness for earning money.[6]

The teacher's plan was so successful that the school recommended Steve skip two grades so he could start learning a foreign language. His parents were reluctant but finally agreed to let him skip fifth grade and to start sixth grade at the middle school.

The school Steve enrolled in had a bad reputation. Many of the students were rowdy or were considered ruffians. A few threatened teachers or jumped from windows just to avoid using the doors. Police were frequently called to break up fights.

It was difficult for Steve to move from a good relationship with an excellent teacher into this rough environment with older students. His sixth-grade report card read, "Steven is an excellent reader. However he wastes much time during reading period. . . . He has great difficulty motivating himself or seeing the purpose of studying reading. . . . He can be a discipline problem at times."[7]

Steve knew he had a problem and told his parents that he would not go back to that school for seventh grade. His parents realized that both his wildness and his intelligence went unnoticed in the middle school. He was a discipline problem at home and at school and was at risk of becoming a juvenile delinquent.[8]

Experiments
and Electronics

During the summer of 1966, the Jobs family moved to the neighboring community of Los Altos. Paul Jobs had moved quickly up through the machinists' ranks and was able to purchase a three-bedroom home with a large attached garage.

In Los Altos, Clara Jobs continued with her part-time job, and Paul kept restoring old cars. Patty started junior high and thirteen-year-old Steve began high school, where, in 1968, work boots and work shirts were the rage with students.

Steve continued with the Mountain View swim team for a while after he entered Homestead High School, but he had been placed in the academic program for gifted students and soon found competitive swimming too time-consuming. He joined the water polo team at his school but quit after being encouraged to knee his opponents in the groin to get an advantage over them.

After his experience with water polo, Steve took up playing the trumpet and joined the high school marching band. The band provided him with a group to belong to, social interactions, and musical experience without competition. He played with the band for only a year before he turned in his trumpet for a guitar and a harmonica. He had taken a strong interest in the music of Bob Dylan, a nationally famous singer, musician, and composer, whose songs reflected social problems of the 1960s. Steve practiced playing and singing like Dylan and started a collection of Bob Dylan memorabilia.

His interest in electronics continued. In his first year of high school, Steve needed some electronic components for a counting device. He called Bill Hewlett, cofounder of Hewlett-Packard, at his home to ask for the parts. They talked for twenty minutes. Steve not only got the electronics he needed, he got a job offer from Hewlett to work on the assembly line during his summer vacation. His job would be to tighten screws in frequency counters. Steve was in heaven.[1]

In middle school, Steve had met Bill Fernandez, and now both were attending Homestead High School. Through their mutual interest in science and electronics, the two became good friends. Bill Fernandez had the best collection of electronic devices that Steve had seen, thanks to a neighbor who was an engineer. With the various relays, transistors, and diodes, the boys tried to build a number of electronic gadgets, but most of their projects took more knowledge than they had.

Bill Fernandez's neighbor had an eighteen-year-old son, Steve Wozniak, who asked Bill to help him design and build a computer. One day Fernandez invited Steve Jobs to see the computer and meet its inventor. Steve was impressed with the computer—and with Steve Wozniak. His computer had won an award in a Bay Area science fair. "He was the first person I met who knew more electronics than I did," said Jobs.[2]

Although the younger boys were just thirteen and

As a teenager, Steve idolized singer Bob Dylan and learned to play some of his songs on the guitar.

fourteen, Wozniak—who liked to be called Woz—gladly interacted with them because of their interest in electronics. He encouraged the two to take the electronics course offered by the high school. In their sophomore year, Steve and Bill enrolled in John McCollum's Electronics I class.

In McCollum's classroom, shelves held thousands of electronic components mostly donated by companies such as Hewlett-Packard. The Homestead High electronics lab had as much test equipment as the local community college and much more than most high schools.[3] McCollum challenged his students. When they finished a project, he would insert a faulty part or disconnect a wire so students had to figure out what was wrong and fix it. It was his way of teaching them to think things through.[4]

Steve Jobs thought things through but in a different way. Once, when he needed but could not afford parts for a project, Steve made a phone call to a company in Detroit, Michigan. He not only talked someone there into giving him the parts for free, he got the phone call for free. He had called collect. When McCollum found out about the collect call, he became angry. Steve replied, "I don't have the money for the phone call. They've got plenty of money."[5]

With their enrollment in electronics and their participation in the school's electronics club, Bill and Steve became "wireheads." It was cool to be a wirehead.[6] They were different from nerds. Wireheads made things, impressed people, and represented the general population of the area soon to be referred to as Silicon Valley. Nerds had the reputation of being smart but unsociable. It was not cool to be a nerd.

Bill Fernandez, like Woz, spent three years studying electronics under McCollum. Steve, however, did not go on after the first year. His interests now included literature and classical music. It did not surprise McCollum when Steve chose to quit after Electronics I. The teacher later said, "He had a different way of looking at things. I'd put him down as something of a loner. He would tend to be over by himself thinking."[7]

Steve did a lot of thinking. He and Fernandez would take long walks and talk about the philosophy of life. They discussed religion, the Vietnam War, drugs, music, and girls. Fernandez remarked, "We used to walk for hours in the evenings. We were both interested in the spiritual side of things, the big questions: Who are we? What is it all about? What does it mean? . . . Mostly it was Steve who would do the talking. I was a very good listener."[8]

The two friends continued their electronics work in Fernandez's garage or Steve's bedroom. Paul Jobs was working at Spectra Physics and provided his son with a multitude of spare parts, including lasers. The boys played loud rock music, positioned mirrors on the stereo speakers, and pointed the lasers at the mirrors. Then they watched lights dance around the room.

Steve continued to participate in the school's electronics club, whose members tried to get the electronics they needed for free. When free parts were not available, they shopped at Haltek, a block-long store that was like an electronics junkyard. They could get almost anything there, even the old-fashioned vacuum tubes that had been replaced by transistors. Steve spent many hours in the store and learned so much about the merchandise that he was offered a job after his sophomore year. He worked at the counter taking orders.

Steve had also learned to find inexpensive parts at flea markets that sold electronics. When he came across some transistors, he used the negotiating skills he had learned from his father. The transistors cost him very little, and he sold them to Haltek for a profit. Steve Wozniak confided, "I thought it was a flaky idea but he knew what he was doing."[9]

In August, right before Steve started his junior year at Homestead High School, he bought, with his father's approval, a red Fiat 850 coupe. It was rather undependable, but he could afford it with the money he had made that summer at Haltek. The following February when he got his driver's license, he visited Woz two or three times a week at the University of California at Berkeley, where Woz was enrolled as a junior engineering student. Steve also spent many hours in the Stanford coffee shop, usually skipping school to do so. He enjoyed this new freedom.

Steve joined the Buck Fry Club, a practical jokers' club. Homestead High tolerated the club as long as the members did not do serious damage or endanger any students. The club gummed up locks on the school's doors. They reset the school's fire alarm system so that it would constantly buzz. Steve Jobs was following in Steve Wozniak's footstep. Woz had earned a reputation as a practical joker on campus a few years before.

After another summer working for Haltek, Steve Jobs returned for his senior year at Homestead High School. He had read Shakespeare, Dylan Thomas, and, as he reported, "all that classic stuff."[10] His English and writing skills were so advanced that he took classes at Stanford, driving his Fiat to and from the college.

His car also provided opportunities for him to spend time with Chris-Ann, his first girlfriend. He drove to school at night to be with her while she worked on an animated movie.

A jazz band practiced down the hall from Chris-Ann, and Steve decided to adapt his laser light show to fit their music and perform with them. Colored laser light danced around the gymnasium in sync with the band's music, intriguing onlookers. Years later many rock groups would use the same technology to provide a focus for their performances.

A former member of the jazz band, Terri Anzur, said of Jobs, "Steve was kind of a brain and kind of a hippie, but he never fit into either group. He was smart enough to be a nerd, but wasn't nerdy, and he was too intellectual for the hippies, who just wanted to get wasted all the time."[11]

Steve Jobs was a thinker and experimenter. He wanted to exaggerate his intellectual appearance, so he began smoking a pipe at sixteen. He also occasionally smoked marijuana, which made him unpopular with his friends, especially Steve Wozniak. Drugs interfere with logical thinking, and Jobs needed to be

In high school, Steve was a "wirehead" who loved to experiment with electronics. He also joined a practical jokers' club and played pranks on his classmates.

thinking straight to work with electronics. Thinking straight was particularly important when he and Woz got into making and selling blue boxes, gadgets just as illegal as drugs.

Blue box was the term given to an electronic device that made it possible to make long-distance telephone calls for free. It imitated the telephone's tones that were used to make connections to any place in the world. An article published in *Esquire* magazine in October 1971 explained how to make it. Not realizing it was illegal, Wozniak's mother mailed the article to her son at Berkeley. Before he had even finished the article, Woz was on the phone to Steve to discuss making a blue box.[12] It was an exciting challenge—not because it was illegal, but because even with their limited electronic skills, they could reproduce it.

They worked several months developing their blue box and were overjoyed when they finally had a design that worked. Steve Jobs said later, "We thought it was absolutely incredible that you could build this little box and make phone calls around the world."[13]

Wozniak's blue box was about the size of a deck of cards and connected directly to the phone line. The first person they called was Woz's grandmother in Los Angeles. The call went through and they yelled into the phone, "It actually works. It actually works. We called you for free."[14] Unfortunately, they had dialed the wrong number and reached a stranger in Los Angeles.

Woz was happy just to have designed the device. Steve Jobs, however, saw an opportunity. He talked

Woz into making more blue boxes so he could sell them. He wanted to buy a new car.

Jobs bought $40 worth of parts for each blue box. Woz initially took four hours to put each one together, but after he designed a printed circuit board and no longer had to solder wires, it took only one hour. Jobs sold the blue box to college students for $150 each and split the profit with Woz. To show off their invention at Homestead High, Jobs used the school pay phones to call Dial-a-Tune in London and to call a recording telling the time in Nepal. Students were invited to listen—compliments of the blue box.

The blue boxes were easy to make, but selling them came at a price. Two customers threatened to turn the pair in to the police rather than pay, so they got the device for free. At another sale, outside a pizza parlor, the customer pulled out a gun and poked it into Jobs's stomach. Jobs was scared: "There were eighteen hundred things I could do but every one had some probability that he would shoot me in the stomach."[15] Jobs turned the blue box over to the armed man.

Jobs and Woz decided to quit on their own, before they got into real trouble. Their final close call came one night when Jobs's Fiat broke down, and the boys took their blue box to a public phone to call for help. A suspicious policeman stopped to question the boys and to search them for drugs. He found the blue box. An interesting conversation followed:

Policeman: What's this?
Wozniak: A music synthesizer.

Policeman: What's this orange button for?
Jobs: Oh, that's for calibration.
Wozniak: It's a computer-controlled synthesizer.
Policeman: Where's the computer, then?
Jobs: That plugs inside.

Neither the policeman nor the boys knew what an electronic music synthesizer looked like, but the explanation seemed plausible. Later in the police car, as they were taken to get help for the broken-down Fiat, the policeman, who had obviously been thinking of the boys' device, said, "Too bad. A guy named Moog beat you to it."

Jobs replied, "Oh, yeah, he sent us the schematics."[16]

Their association with blue boxes was over, but not before they had made more than $6,000 selling the illegal devices.

By the end of his senior year in high school, Steve Jobs had grown tall and thin. He experimented with various diets and sleep deprivation. He grew his hair long and stopped shaving. He rented a cabin in the woods that summer, using money from the sale of blue boxes. Chris-Ann joined him there, and they seemed to have an idyllic existence sitting in the sun, playing the guitar, and eating as they pleased. But it did not last long.

One afternoon while Steve was driving down the mountain from his cabin, the Fiat developed an electrical short and caught on fire. Paul Jobs had the car towed to his house in Los Altos. Steve had to pay for the repairs.

Along with his two best friends, Steve got a job. For $3 an hour, Steve, Chris-Ann, and Woz dressed up as fairy-tale characters from *Alice in Wonderland*. They traipsed up and down the halls of a local mall, entertaining children for four hours a day. Chris-Ann played Alice, and the boys took turns being the Mad Hatter and the White Rabbit. The costumes were hot and bulky, and children sometimes treated them impolitely. It was not a fairy-tale job.

Free Spirit

When it came time to apply to colleges, Steve decided that the only school he wanted to attend was Reed College in Portland, Oregon. He had seen enough of Stanford, which struck him as a bit old-fashioned, and the University of California at Berkeley, which he thought was too big.

Reed was a small liberal arts college that offered a lot of exposure to liberal ideas. Tuition was high, but Steve told his parents that it was Reed College or no college. When he was accepted, his parents finally agreed to make the financial sacrifice, and in September 1972 they drove their son to Portland to begin his college career. Jobs admitted that his parting with his parents at college was not cordial. "I sort of said, 'Well, thanks, 'bye.' I didn't even want the buildings to see that my parents were there. I didn't even want parents at that time. . . . I just wanted to find out what life was all about."[1]

In 1972, Reed College had twelve hundred students. One of Jobs's college friends, Elizabeth Holmes, later said, "In the early seventies Reed was a campus of loners and freaks."[2] Jobs's hair was long, lank, and stringy. He wore torn pants and shirts, and because he seldom showered, he usually smelled bad. He went barefoot except when it snowed. Then he wore Birkenstock sandals. He lived in a coed dormitory, which was unusual at that time, and enrolled in a dance class to meet girls.

His best friend at Reed was Dan Kottke. The two young men discussed philosophical questions, ate vegetarian meals because the regular meals in the cafeteria were not to their liking, and grew interested in Far Eastern religions, including Hinduism and Buddhism. Their vacations were spent at the Oregon shore, where the rising tide would soak their sleeping bags.

Reed was a challenging college, and although Jobs had succeeded in academic classes the previous year at Stanford, he did not care for the demands at Reed and dropped out after his first semester. About a third of the students at Reed dropped out before their senior year, but Jobs dropped out before his eighteenth birthday, the age when most students are just starting college.

Jobs's parents were disappointed that he quit college, and they stopped sending him money to live on. He continued to live in the dormitory even though he was no longer an official resident. He just settled into any vacant room as residents came and went.[3] Jobs spent his days attending classes, although he neither paid the fees nor received credit for the classes.

Jobs and Kottke were attracted to the Hare Krishna, a religious cult established in India in 1954, because of the group's Sunday feast. The members would sit through a lecture, take part in dancing and chanting, and finally eat a large vegetarian meal. It was the only full meal Jobs would have during the week, and he usually took home leftovers.

Steve Jobs constantly needed money. He decided to sell his electric typewriter so he would have money to buy food and incense for a couple of months. Robert Friedland bought the typewriter. He was several years older than Jobs, dressed in robes from India, and was Reed's student body president. He was an outgoing, friendly guy who taught Jobs a lot about selling, coming out of his shell, and opening up and taking charge of any situation.

At the end of the school year, when he could no longer stay in the dormitory, Jobs rented an unheated room near the college for $25 a month. He had been a vegetarian for more than a year, but he continued to experiment with his diet. For several months, due mostly to his financial situation, he ate only Roman Meal cereal and milk taken from the dining hall. A box would last him one week. He said later, "After three months of Roman Meal I was just going out of my gourd."[4]

After a few months Jobs decided he needed a regular income. He was hired by the Psychology Department at Reed College to maintain its electronic equipment. He was only eighteen, and except for what he had learned in McCollum's course at Homestead High, he had little formal education in electronics. Ron Fial, an assistant professor, said, "He was very good. He often didn't want to just fix something. He often ended up bringing in something that was completely redesigned."[5]

Steve had attended lectures and read books about Zen Buddhism and became interested in Eastern philosophy. He needed a place to meditate, but his rented room was uncomfortably cold during the winter. He furnished the crawl space above Kottke's

A Hare Krishna festival: Jobs and his friend Dan were drawn to this religious cult, which started in India. They liked the big vegetarian Sunday feasts.

dormitory room with a rug so he could burn incense and meditate. He found meditation to be more fulfilling than any drug he had tried, because meditation took him to a higher awareness in a natural way. He was trying to find out who he was. He wanted to comprehend his universe.[6]

Zen Buddhism encourages fasting, and Jobs believed that fasts were necessary for well-being. However, as he did with other things, he took his fasting to an extreme. He would not eat for a couple of weeks, or he would eat only specific foods such as carrots, which made his skin turn orange. He was a close observer of how his eating affected his body and said of his fasting experiences, "After a few days you start to feel great. After a week you start to feel fantastic. You get a ton of vitality from not having to digest all this food."[7]

Jobs's friend Robert Friedland had made a pilgrimage to India and now operated a three-hundred-acre Oregon farm that was owned by wealthy relatives. He turned it into a commune, and Steve Jobs visited frequently. Residents of the farm lived cooperatively, grew most of their own food, and meditated. Jobs and Friedland discussed India and the country's spiritual issues. Consequently, Jobs became obsessed with traveling to India.

In the spring of 1974, soon after he turned nineteen, Steve Jobs moved back to his parents' house in Los Altos. He had no money and was looking for a job when an advertisement caught his eye: "Have fun and make money."[8] He wanted money for a trip to India, so he went for an interview. When the receptionist at

Atari saw Steve Jobs, she called the chief engineer and said, "We've got this kid in the lobby. He's either a crackpot or he's got something."[9] Jobs proceeded to persuade the company president to hire him.

Atari had become a big name in electronic games with its invention of Pong, a revolutionary game Jobs played often. Pong connected to a television set, with one or two players hitting an electronic ball back and forth, much like table tennis.

Atari was constantly developing new games. Steve Jobs was employee number forty in a company that would eventually hire thousands. He fine-tuned electronic chips to make improvements in the games and earned $5 an hour, more than twice the minimum wage at that time.

Jobs was the only employee who worked at night. He had recently settled on a diet that included fasting and excluded meat, alcohol, fat, bread, potatoes, rice, and milk. He ate large quantities of figs, nuts, green onions, grated horseradish, and honey. The inventor of this diet told participants that these foods eliminated mucus and other wastes from the body, so participants no longer needed to bathe.[10] Steve Jobs believed it, but his coworkers had a different opinion.

Jobs let Woz come in and keep him company at night. While Jobs worked, Woz would play an Atari driving game, stopping only to help his friend with technical problems.[11]

Dan Kottke dropped out of Reed College before his senior year, and in the spring of 1974 he moved in with Steve and his parents. Dan slept on the couch at night and walked the streets of Silicon Valley during the day. Steve tried to get him a job at Atari, but Kottke had no skills. For entertainment, Dan would also come to Atari at night, playing games and keeping his friend company. Unlike Woz, however, Kottke could not help Steve with any of his work.

For three years Jobs and Kottke had been planning to go to India to study more about Eastern philosophy. Jobs finally decided they should go in the summer of 1975 and asked Atari to pay his way.

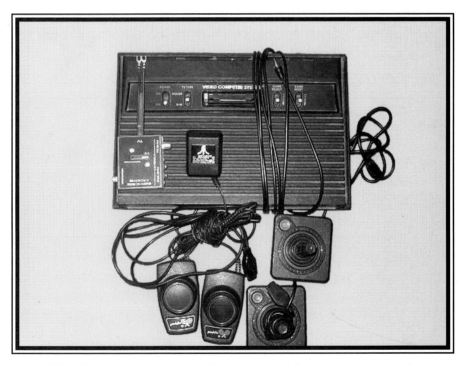

This Atari game set was played on a television screen. Jobs started working for Atari after answering an ad that read, "Have fun and make money."

Atari refused but did agree to send him to Germany to fix some problems the company was having with German electrical power. Atari also agreed that Jobs could have vacation time to pursue his interests in India. After fixing the power problem in Germany— it took only two hours—Steve Jobs was on his way to India.

India, Insights, and Inventions

In New Delhi, India, twenty-year-old Steve Jobs witnessed poverty such as he had never seen before. But despite the homelessness, starvation, and illness, the Indian people appeared to Jobs to be happy. They had faith that something better was to come. If followers of Buddhism and Hinduism remained detached from all desires and worldly things, they would be rewarded in a higher life.

Arriving three weeks before Kottke, Jobs wandered around, giving away his possessions. He dressed like the people he saw, in cotton pants and vest, and he usually went barefoot because his crude sandals rubbed his feet raw. Sometimes he wore only a *lunghi*, the traditional loincloth of spiritual men. He ate whatever food was available and slept wherever he felt comfortable.

One day, while Jobs was walking in the Himalayas, the smell of food attracted him to a religious festival. He joined the feasting crowd and was surprised when the *baba*, the holy man of this festival, stood in front of him and burst out laughing. Steve Jobs later said, "Then he grabbed my arm and took me up this mountain trail. It was a little funny, because here were hundreds of Indians who had traveled for thousands of miles to hang out with this guy for ten seconds, and I stumble in for something to eat and he's dragging me up this mountain path."[1] At the

Jobs's spiritual journey took him to India in 1975. This photo shows the Taj Mahal, a famous tomb built in the 1600s.

top of the mountain was a pond. The *baba* dunked Jobs's head in the water, pulled out a razor, and shaved his head. Jobs was never given an explanation, though he noticed that many of those around him also had shaved heads.

When Kottke arrived in New Delhi, the two friends set out to find the headwaters of the Ganges River. They followed the great waterway north and into the Himalayas, passing temples, festivals, religious ceremonies, clothes washing, and body washing. The muddy brown water, sacred to many, attracted people from all over the Hindu world. The water was said to cure ailments, cleanse and purify the body, and carry those who died in it to Paradise. Flaming funeral rafts carried the dead downstream with the current. Countless beggars came to the river each day to die in its waters, contributing decaying bodies to a river already contaminated with human waste and disease. But the young Americans were enticed farther up the river by holy men sitting cross-legged on rock ledges, by brightly colored banners, and by the smell of incense, saffron, herbs, tea, and lotus flowers.

During this adventure up the Ganges, Jobs and Kottke had planned to stop in Kainchi, the home of Neem Karoli Baba, the guru they had met while at Reed College. They found the community but could find little evidence of the great guru—just a few plastic trinkets and worthless mementos. He had died in 1973, and his followers had moved on.

The young men drifted around India, talking and reading philosophy, taking it all very seriously.[2] They rented a one-room concrete hut from a farmer, whose

Jobs and his friend Dan Kottke set out to find the headwaters of the great Ganges River.

wife sold them water-buffalo milk mixed with sugar. Within a month Jobs was convinced that she was watering down the milk, and after an argument with the woman, the two left.[3]

They decided to visit a guru who lived about ten miles away, up a dry riverbed. The trail was almost impossible to follow, winding over and between boulders, but the men eventually came across a stairway leading up the cliff to the holy man's retreat.

The guru was not what they had expected. Instead of practicing meditation and philosophy, the guru changed his clothes frequently and talked in flowery language. The young men were not impressed. They cut their visit short, leaving the cliff one afternoon just hours before a roaring rainstorm hit.

From April to October is monsoon season in India. The rainstorms strike with little notice and can dump twelve inches of rain in a matter of hours. The riverbed Steve Jobs and Dan Kottke walked in had been dry because the seasonal rains had not yet filled the river with new water. Mountains towered around them, and when the monsoon hit, rainwater rushed from the mountains, down dry gullies, and into the river. Jobs and Kottke were trapped in the torrential downpour. As the water level rose, the friends feared a flash flood would wipe them out. They huddled together and prayed. In fear and in prayer they survived the night of lightning, thunder, howling wind, and pelting rain.[4]

Their interest in India was not the same after that rainy night. They both were suffering from a number of health problems, and Kottke's traveler's checks had been stolen. When his friend could not collect on a claim against his stolen checks, Jobs gave Kottke $300 and went home. Kottke returned to the United States a few weeks later.

Jobs moved back in with his parents. In shaved head and saffron-colored robe, he approached Atari founder Nolan Bushnell about resuming his job. Bushnell liked Jobs's work ethic—the more quickly you could do something, the better he liked you— and hired him back. Jobs asked for a promotion to engineer, with more money and more prestige. Bushnell agreed, as long as Jobs would work nights so he would not offend other engineers with his lack of formal education and his unusual personal habits. Then Jobs requested additional time off so he could visit Kottke in Oregon.

Steve Jobs had a natural curiosity about his adoption and cautiously confided to Kottke that he had hired a private investigator to track down his biological parents. Kottke recommended that his anxious friend attend the Primal Therapy Center in Eugene, Oregon. Jobs paid $1,000 for twelve weeks of therapy. He was put in a soundproof dark box, where he would meditate and then scream until exhausted. He would then share with the group any insights he had developed while in the box. Steve Jobs believed that the therapy gave him no great understanding of his problems, but friends saw a change. They said that he appeared to be giving more thought to how his words might affect other people.[5]

The private investigator was able to track down Jobs's biological parents. After receiving the report, Jobs told only a few people what he had learned. Sometime after he was given up for adoption, his parents had married. They both taught at a university, and he had a biological sister, Mona Simpson. Mona attended the University of California at Berkeley and eventually became a novelist. (Steve and Mona developed a close relationship, and in 1987 she dedicated her first novel, *Anywhere But Here*, to her mother and her brother, Steve Jobs.)[6]

By the time Jobs returned from Oregon and

started back to work at Atari, his hair and beard had started to grow. He had turned in his saffron-colored robe for a pair of jeans with the knees completely ripped out. He resumed his fruitarian diet, took few showers, and continued to work nights because his personal habits still irritated some people. He was placed on a team to design Breakout, a game that uses a ball to destroy a brick wall. But Jobs worked alone at night, so when he had a problem he would call Woz to come in and make everything work.

Meanwhile, Jobs had started attending the Los Altos Zen Center, which seemed to fulfill his spiritual needs. There he ran into Chris-Ann, his girlfriend from high school. They became friends again, and as Chris-Ann made plans for a year in India, Jobs gave her some hard-learned advice.[7]

When the design for Breakout was completed, Jobs took a trip to the All-One Farm, the commune that his friend Robert Friedland had started. The farm had begun to attract drifters, beggars, drug users, members of the Hare Krishna temples, and, on one occasion, patients from a nearby mental hospital. Jobs was no longer comfortable on the farm, so when he finished managing the apple harvest, he left.

Back at his parents' house, Jobs worked occasionally for Atari but spent a lot of time with his friend Steve Wozniak. Woz was involved in designing a computer, which he showed off at Homebrew Computer Club meetings for computer hobbyists. Still fascinated by electronics, Jobs occasionally attended meetings. He would watch the intensity of the hobbyists as they

Jobs spent a summer overseeing the harvesting of apples.

developed electronic components into more and more complex computers. Every hobbyist at the meetings thought he needed a computer. Steve Jobs thought differently: He thought everyone in the country would need one as soon as technology made it possible. He talked Woz into starting a business. They would refine and market his design, intending eventually for their company to place a desktop computer in every household, school, and business.

Steve Jobs had left the apple orchard but was now involved with a company he hoped he could nurture to produce computers as he had nurtured his trees to produce fruit.

6

Apple:
The First Byte

To form a company, Steve Jobs
and Steve Wozniak needed money. The two came up
with a plan. Woz would sell his Hewlett-Packard
programmable calculator for $500. He wanted the
newer model anyway. Jobs would make a bigger
sacrifice; he would sell his red-and-white Volkswagen
van. He would have to ride his bike for a while, but he
would have $1,300 to start a business.

Things did not turn out as planned, however. Two
weeks after the van was sold, the buyer complained
that it needed a new engine, so Jobs refunded $300.
The person who bought the calculator had paid half
the money when he picked it up but decided not to
pay Woz the other half. Together Jobs and Woz had
$1,250, not enough to buy the necessary printed

circuit boards. They went ahead with their plans, thinking somehow they would get the rest of the money.

They had to make many decisions even before they filed the papers for their business. First they needed a name. Other computer companies had names like Sphere, Golemics, Itty Bitty Machine Company, and Kentucky Fried Computer. Jobs and Wozniak considered technical-sounding names like Executek or Matrix Electronics. As their list grew and shrank, one name never changed—Apple. After all, Jobs had been an apple grower at the All-One Farm, and the fruit was one of his favorites. The two worried that people might not take the name Apple seriously, but they liked the idea that *Apple* would come before *Atari* in the phone book. One day Jobs finally said, "Unless we come up with something better by 5:00 P.M. tomorrow, we'll go with Apple."[1] The next day at five, Apple was still at the top of their list.

Another major decision was to take on a third partner. Jobs worried that two people having equal power could run into problems making decisions. So, originally, there were three founders of Apple Computer: Steve Wozniak, Steve Jobs, and Ron Wayne. Jobs knew Wayne from Atari. He was an experienced engineer who had once owned his own company. The agreement signed on April 1, 1976, divided the company three ways. Jobs and Woz would each get 45 percent. Wayne would have 10 percent and would have the tie-breaking vote if Jobs and Woz could not agree on something.

Each person had specific tasks. Wozniak would

design the computers, Wayne would design the logo and write the instruction manual, and Jobs would do the buying and marketing. Any of the partners could write a check for less than $100. For a greater amount, two signatures were required.

Since they were still short the money needed to have the printed circuit boards made, Jobs persuaded an artist at Atari to design and manufacture the boards at a little less than the going rate. Now they had a product to sell. Soon after, the Byte Shop ordered fifty Apple I computers, and the three men were into a frantic routine of designing, building, and delivering.

Wayne had finished his logo, which featured Sir Isaac Newton sitting under an apple tree, and he was well into the development of the instruction manual when the Byte Shop's order was received. He decided this obligation was more than what he had anticipated, and the risk was too great. Although he would be happy to own 10 percent of a successful company, he did not want the 10 percent liability of a failing company. He asked to be released from his obligations after a few months, and he has said he never regretted it.[2] Wayne was forty-one years old and figured he had a promising career at Atari.

Jobs and Wozniak forged ahead without Wayne. When it was time to start production of the Apple I, Patty (Steve's sister), Bill Fernandez, and a couple of high school boys were hired to put the computers together. Another friend would be the accountant.

Patty was married and expecting her first child. She worked at her parents' house, where Steve had taken over her room. She sat on the living room floor watching television as she pushed components into circuit boards. She earned $1 for each assembled board and could make four per hour, so she earned almost as much as Jobs had made at Atari. But television was distracting and sometimes she made mistakes. So Jobs had to spend extra time fixing the defective boards.

Bill Fernandez and the students soldered the boards whenever they could: after school, at night, and on weekends. Woz worked on his dining room table, revising the BASIC program for the Apple I and designing and redesigning the electronics. Jobs looked for better deals on components, talked people into making him things for less, and built up their business until it took over his dad's garage as well as the two bedrooms. Steve's father had always supported his son's ideas, no matter how strange they might be. He not only remodeled the garage for the computer business, he added on a family room to accommodate some of the overflow. Then he built a second garage behind the house for his cars.

The Apple computers were delivered to the Byte Shop within the thirty-day deadline, and the new company had $8,000. Steve Jobs was impressed with the way the business was going, but he worried that he was drifting away from meditation and spirituality into mainstream society. He seriously considered giving it all up to live in a monastery. He consulted with a Zen monk, who said that he would likely find business to be the same as sitting in a monastery, so he should pursue business.[3] Being so advised, Jobs immediately plunged the company deeper into debt, hoping to make an even larger profit.

Each computer cost about $250 to make, so Jobs factored in a profit to the Byte Shop and a profit to Apple and came up with a selling price of $777.77. Woz vetoed that price, saying it was much too high, so they decided on $666.66. Some people who had seen the movie *The Omen* that year thought 666 had an evil significance. Jobs made up the explanation that he took two spiritual numbers, 77777 and 11111, and subtracted; the price had nothing to do with evil.[4]

Their first advertisement said the Apple I computer was available in most computer stores. Most of the seventy-five Byte Shops had an Apple I in their inventory, but they were not selling well. Eventually, 200 Apple I computers were made, but only 150 sold. The rest were gathering dust on Byte Shop shelves.

While the young helpers worked putting the Apple I together, Jobs kept up with the sales, oversaw the advertising, and looked for new customers. Wozniak kept working on the BASIC program, coming up with a new version every few days for Jobs to deliver to the Byte Shops. He also worked on the design for a new computer, the Apple II.

When Woz said that he had an idea for a better computer, Jobs immediately started planning for its production. This could be the computer that ordinary people would buy, not just hobbyists. If things went well, the Apple II could be in every home, helping people with numerous household duties.

The world's first computer festival was to be held Labor Day weekend, 1976, in Atlantic City, New

When Woz, left, said he had an idea for a better computer, Jobs immediately started planning for its production. Jobs imagined a computer for ordinary people, not just technology geeks.

Jersey. Jobs wanted to be there. The company had very little money, so the two men took an all-night flight to Atlantic City, where they joined Kottke. Dressed in jeans and sandals, they set up a booth at the back of the demonstration hall. A card table held their merchandise. Yellow curtains formed a backdrop, while black-and-white signs invited observers to their display. The three men planned to tell the whole world about their computers, but very few people of importance visited the back of the hall. Most people stopped to talk with companies that had prime display areas by the front door.

Jobs and Woz decided the Apple II had to be an easy-to-use machine with programs that would fit into everyday life. It would cost much more than the Apple I, but it would be ready to use as soon as the box was opened.

Jobs figured it would take $1,000 to provide each Apple II computer with case, keyboard, electronics, and a connection for a color monitor. The biggest advance would be that it would use Woz's newly invented floppy disk drive instead of a magnetic tape and cassette recorder, making access to information much faster.[5]

Jobs decided the best way to raise money to design and manufacture the Apple II would be to sell the company. Atari and Hewlett-Packard had already turned down the opportunity to purchase their technology in the spring. But now, in the fall of 1976, Apple I had made an impression on the technical community, and Commodore Business Machines was considering buying Apple. Jobs said he wanted

$100,000 for the company. He also wanted Commodore stock and salaries for himself and Woz of $36,000 a year, double what most college-educated people were making at that time. Commodore withdrew the offer. The chairman of the board thought it was absurd to acquire two guys with a business in a garage.[6]

Jobs looked elsewhere for money. He invited several venture capitalists to invest in Apple. Venture capitalists are wealthy people who invest money in young or expanding companies, hoping to make money as the company grows. Because a new company is at risk for failing, the investors agree to provide money in exchange for part ownership of the company.

Mike Markkula showed up at Jobs's garage one day to look into the company and was impressed with what he saw—a couple of guys serious about a new product. Markkula had made enough money with Intel stock to retire in his early thirties. Now he had money to invest, experience in electronics, and need of a hobby or some other pursuit to keep him active. Jobs and Woz were thrilled when he made them an offer. In exchange for 30 percent interest in Apple, Mike Markkula would draw up the business plans, invest $91,000 of his own money, arrange for a $250,000 line of credit, and devote four years to building the business. He thought he was just giving advice to two sharp kids.[7]

Jobs was excited. He was willing to give Markkula 30 percent of Apple, not just for the investment, but also for the experience that came with the new partner. Here was a man he could learn from.

Markkula moved the company out of the garage and into a building in Cupertino, and on January 3, 1977, incorporation papers were signed. Markkula, Wozniak, and Jobs would each have 30 percent of Apple and draw salaries of $20,000 a year. Ron Holt, an engineer Woz described as the greatest designer in the universe, would have 10 percent. Their first challenge was getting the Apple II ready to be introduced and sold at the West Coast Computer Faire in San Francisco in April.

Designs, Details, and Dinners

$\mathbf{S}$teve Jobs often had a tough time meeting deadlines because he was difficult to please and sometimes made more changes than the project had allotted time for. He considered himself an artist, designing and redesigning computer cases, artfully negotiating and renegotiating better prices for materials, and preparing and giving increasingly innovative presentations to customers and investors.

Jobs knew that the looks of the Apple II would attract the nontechnical people he was trying to impress. All other computers were made from sheet metal; Jobs decided he wanted a sleek plastic case.[1]

The case had to have a removable lid, be high enough to house the electronics, and be big enough so that it would not overheat. Jobs offered Jerry

Mannock, an engineer turned designer, $1,500 for making mechanical drawings for a case. Mannock, who wondered whether he should work with such flaky-looking people, managed to satisfy Jobs's demands.

Two molding processes were available for the cases. Thinking that only five thousand Apple II computers would be manufactured and sold, Jobs went with the less expensive method. When the first cases were received, just days before the West Coast Computer Faire, Jobs found that they were rickety. The surfaces were uneven and the air vents were not cleanly cut. Apple employees worked frantically to turn the eyesores into attractive cases. They trimmed edges with sharp knives, filled dents with putty, smoothed all surfaces with sandpaper, and spray painted the cases to give them a finished look. Then the cases were stuffed with electronics and the Apple II was ready to be introduced to the world.

Steve Jobs had signed up for the West Coast Computer Faire early so that Apple could have a space directly opposite the main entrance, not in the back where few serious computer buyers wandered. Markkula ordered a large, smoky, back-lit plastic sign with the new Apple logo to hang behind them. Counters draped in dark cloth rather than card tables would display the three computers and stacks of brochures, while a large television would demonstrate the computer's features. The dozen Apple employees would dress nicely, not in jeans and sandals. Steve Jobs would be shaved, groomed, and wearing his first three-piece suit.

Everything worked. Apple Computer Company had spent $10,000 to participate in the computer fair, but many times that amount was made. The company sold more than three hundred Apple computers.

Steve Jobs had trouble giving up decision-making control of Apple Computer, but he agreed with Markkula that Apple needed a president. They hired Michael M. Scott, who ended up fighting Jobs for control. The company now had five prominent people: Markkula, chairman of the board; Wozniak, head computer designer; Holt, head engineer; Scott, president; and Jobs with no official position except vice chairman. Jobs had difficulty fitting in.

After becoming president in May 1977, one of the first decisions that Scott made was to give every employee a number. Jobs was given number two. When he found out that Scott had given Woz number one because he had invented the computer, Jobs insisted on being employee number zero instead of number two.[2] His identification badge said employee zero, but for bookkeeping purposes Jobs remained number two.

"A is for Apple" read an advertisement from the 1970s.

Scott was hired as

president for $20,001 a year—one dollar more than the three major shareholders—but he did not have the voting power of the founders. He and Jobs were constantly arguing about who would sign purchase orders, how materials should be moved and stored, and how the furniture should be arranged. When Scott was asked what he thought of Jobs, he said, "Jobs cannot run anything. He doesn't know how to manage people. After you get something started he causes lots of waves. He likes to fly around like a hummingbird at ninety miles per hour. He needs to be sat on."[3]

Jobs was like a hummingbird. With no official job and no real responsibility, he flitted from project to project, desk to desk, sometimes ruffling feathers and generally making himself unpopular, sometimes inspiring work that seemed impossible.

Publicity and advertising were important to the growth of the computer industry, and Steve Jobs wanted a superior ad campaign. After researching public relations agencies, he selected Regis McKenna Agency. Jobs had been very impressed with the Intel ads the small firm had produced. He called Regis McKenna several times a day before he finally reached him. A meeting date was set, and Jobs decided he would not leave McKenna's office without an agreement.

Jobs took Wozniak along to the first meeting with Regis McKenna. Woz had with him an article he was writing for *Dr. Dobb's Journal of Computing*. McKenna was curious about the piece and asked to see it. Much to Jobs's surprise, a sensitive Wozniak blurted out, "I don't want any PR man touching my copy!"[4]

McKenna was insulted and wanted them both out, but Jobs was not ready to leave. He did not have an agreement yet. He calmed them both down. Then, with his personable manner, Jobs convinced McKenna that Apple was a rapidly growing company with a superb product, and everyone would benefit greatly from their association. McKenna finally agreed and the two left.

McKenna's art director decided that the logo Ron Wayne had drawn was too complicated for small reproductions. He developed the silhouette of an apple in rainbow-striped colors with a bite taken out of it. He said, "I wanted to simplify the shape of an apple, and by taking a bite—a byte, right?—out of the side, it prevented the apple from looking like a cherry tomato."[5] The bite represented the computer term *byte*. Byte is the name for the unit of computer memory it takes to store a single character.

One of the first McKenna ads showed a woman working in the kitchen while her husband sat at the table using an Apple II computer. The copy read, "The home computer that's ready to work, play and grow with you. . . . You'll be able to organize, index and store data on household finances, income taxes, recipes, your biorhythms, balance your checking account, even control your home environment."[6] McKenna was selling Steve Jobs's belief that eventually everyone would want a computer.

While the Apple II was in development, Steve Jobs had found only one company that made the components essential to the new circuit board. The company insisted that Apple pay full price, so Jobs requested a face-to-face meeting. Wozniak went along, and when

Steve Jobs outside Apple headquarters. The company logo then was a rainbow-colored apple with a "byte" taken out of the side.

the company refused to offer a discount, Jobs threatened to pull his business from the firm. Again Jobs was surprised by his partner, who said innocently, "But these are the only guys who can make the parts that will work."[7]

Jobs kicked Woz under the table to shut him up. A comment like that would not help in bargaining for a better price. Then Jobs slipped off his chair onto the floor beneath the table. The sales manager still refused to cut the price, but he was amused by Jobs's disappearing act and offered them a $40,000 line of credit for thirty days. Apple could get the components but not have to pay for them for thirty days. Once again Steve Jobs's personality got him what he wanted.

When the Apple II went into production, Jobs went looking for programs that could be run on the new computer. He encouraged new owners of the Apple II to write programs, mostly games, and paid them according to how many lines of code they used. He paid one programmer $50 for a program that had only two lines of code.[8] Very happy with the programmer, Jobs hired him permanently.

Jobs spent most of his time at Apple and very little time at his new residence. During the summer of 1977, Jobs, his high school sweetheart Chris-Ann, and Dan Kottke rented a house. None of the three had many possessions, since they had all been living with parents, so the house remained mostly empty. Jobs furnished his room with a mattress, a meditation cushion, and a single picture on the wall. His few clothes were kept in boxes.

Kottke slept on a foam pad next to an old piano in the living room because he had turned his bedroom into a neighborhood attraction. He filled the small room thigh-deep with fist-size chunks of foam packing material and let the neighborhood kids play in it. Chris-Ann disliked living in the house and moved out after a few months.

As 1977 was drawing to a close, more than 2,500 Apple II computers had been sold. In September of that year, the strain of production had caused the machine that made the case to fail. Jobs took advantage of this opportunity to switch to the more expensive but more reliable process. He flew to Portland, Oregon, to talk to a prominent plastic tooling maker who was unsure that it would be worth the time and money to work with a small company like Apple. Besides, the schedule seemed impossible to meet. Jobs knew this was the only company that could do the work properly, so he offered a bonus of $1,000 a week for every week ahead of schedule. The company agreed and delivered the cases early.

All through 1977 the two dozen Apple employees worked in a space smaller than an average home. Partitions separated the offices from the assembly area. All the offices were the same; a space for a desk but little more. The president's cubicle was just like all the others. Half the manufacturing space was used to store three years' worth of high-quality plastic that Jobs had gotten in bulk at an excellent price.

In spite of the small space, everything was new and everyone was enthusiastic. No routines were needed in the first building because people usually came to work before 8:00 A.M. and stayed until late in the evening. Some worked all night, taking naps in sleeping bags on the floor. Jobs thrived on the schedule.

Their move at the beginning of 1978 to the new building, Bandley One, meant important people would have their own offices. Jobs and Scott would have walls and doors between them, but the walls did not stop the disagreements. In fact, for his twenty-third birthday several weeks after the move, Jobs found in his office a funeral wreath of white roses with a card saying RIP (rest in peace) signed by the president.

Jobs was officially the vice president of research and development, and he usually made rounds each day to check on the progress of various projects. He would compliment and encourage some workers but anger others. He was a perfectionist who so frequently rejected employees' work that behind his back they called him "The Rejecter."[9]

One routine left unchanged by the move was the late-night pizza get-togethers. Those working through dinner, usually employees who were single or had no children, would assemble at a local pizza parlor for pineapple pizza and continue work-related discussions. This became such a tradition that during interviews, potential employees were asked if they liked pineapple pizza. A no could mean the person would not be hired because, as employee Chris Espinosa said, "How could they come out to dinner with us?"[10] Dinner was part of the workday.

In May 1978 Steve Jobs drove to Oregon to see Chris-Ann at the All-One Farm. She had moved there after leaving the house she shared with Jobs and Kottke and now had a baby girl. She told Jobs that he was the father, but he refused to accept that. He gave her no money to help raise the baby, but he did want to participate in her naming. He knew many children in the commune had unusual names. He thought Chris-Ann's baby should have a normal name. Together they agreed on the name Lisa.

Not only was Apple Computer Company changing in 1979, Steve Jobs's life was changing. He had started work on a new computer, the Apple III, but still received an average salary, not enough to buy the expensive things he wanted. So he sold a million dollars' worth of his stock options to purchase a BMW motorcycle, a Mercedes coupe with no leather (because of his vegetarian beliefs), and a large home in Los Altos.

He still had no time or inclination to furnish the house. Even his current girlfriend, a woman who worked at the McKenna Agency, could not persuade him to decorate it. The kitchen was fully furnished, but architectural plans littered other rooms. In his bedroom he had an Apple II, a mattress, and a dresser with pictures of former California governor Jerry Brown, Albert Einstein, and Neem Karoli Baba, the guru he and Kottke had hoped to meet in India. A bookcase was half filled with books, and the dining room table had few chairs. Whenever people came over for dinner, Jobs had to borrow chairs from neighbors.

Meanwhile, sales of the Apple II continued to climb. During 1978, eight thousand were sold. The next year thirty-five thousand were sold, and the company was worth $47 million. The partners were thinking of taking the company public. That meant stock would be sold outside the company, and anyone buying stock could make a lot of money if Apple Computer Company continued to grow.

To prepare for going public, Apple president Michael Scott reorganized the company. Jobs had been the unofficial head of one of the new computer projects and was expecting to be a divisional manager, but his name was not on the list. In fact, it was not on any list. His feelings were hurt and he was furious.[11]

Other computers of the time were housed in sheet metal, but Jobs wanted a sleek plastic case for the Apple II.

Scott told him what he really thought: that Jobs lacked the experience and the temperament to be a divisional manager. Then he told Jobs that his skills were needed to help with the public stock offering. As he often did, Steve Jobs invited an employee to join him on a long walk. The colleague listened as Jobs talked about his job prospects with Apple Computer. It looked as if he would have little to do.

Youngest of
the Superrich

Steve Jobs, regardless of his relationships with staff, helped Apple Computer Company grow significantly, and finally, on December 12, 1980, the company went public. On that day Jobs and many other Apple employees became multimillionaires. All management staff had been given stock options, which they could now cash in. Being a company founder, Steve Jobs had 7.5 million shares of Apple stock now valued at $29 per share. That meant Jobs was worth more than $200 million. At twenty-five, he instantly became the youngest of the superrich.[1] He thought about celebrating by sharing the cost of a private jet with Markkula but decided not to be such a showoff.

Instead, he celebrated by buying a bottle of wine—a $200 bottle of wine.

Not everybody working at Apple became rich that day. The hourly employees—the technicians, the assemblers, the shippers—had not received corporate stock as part of their employment package. This meant that Bill Fernandez (employee number 4), Chris Espinosa (employee number 8) and Dan Kottke (employee number 12) had no stock options because they were not part of the management team. Some people at Apple felt bad about this, but Steve Jobs insisted that the policy be consistent: Although these three had been with the company since the beginning, they were hourly, and like all other nonmanagers, they should not be given stock options.

A few managers, Markkula and Wozniak among them, believed the three were deserving of stock and arranged to give them some shares. The stock did not put the three into the millionaire bracket, but it was enough to let them know they were acknowledged as major building blocks of the business.

Steve Jobs used $1.6 million of his new wealth to build a Spanish-style mansion in Los Gatos. He barraged the contractors with his demands, and when it was finished, the house had no more furniture than his other houses. The empty rooms were dark, but outside were a long private driveway, a well that provided water to the property, and seven acres of woodlands. He could take long walks on his own property and meditate in the privacy of nature.

Jobs was uncomfortable with his riches, though. He wanted to help his parents but was worried that

Young and superrich, Jobs built himself a mansion in California, but he still lived simply without a clutter of furniture.

he would unintentionally upset their lifestyle. He worried that women might like him just for his money, and he knew that his friends expected him to use his money wisely. "You run out of things to buy real quick," he said.[2] He always had a nice car, but in general the money did not change his daily life much. He still wore jeans and sandals, although he purchased more business suits; he still ate vegetarian meals; and he still spent most of his hours working for Apple.

The sales of the Apple II continued to increase, and three new computer models had been proposed in 1979: the Apple III, the Macintosh, and the Lisa, which many people think was named after Jobs's daughter.

In 1979 Xerox Corporation let Jobs and a few others see their labs in exchange for being given permission to buy a million dollars' worth of Apple stock. The agreement benefited both companies. Apple stock eventually rose 1,600 percent, giving Xerox a $15-million profit. Xerox had shown Apple a program that ran with overlapping windows and pop-up menus controlled by a mouse. Xerox had no immediate interest in using its point-and-click computer device. Jobs, on the other hand, saw the future. He immediately assigned a team of computer engineers to develop similar technology so the Lisa and the Macintosh could be mouse-operated.

In late 1980 the Apple III was shipped. Jobs had wanted a machine that had no fan so users would not be disturbed by the constant noise. But sometimes when components of the Apple III overheated, they

worked their way out of their sockets. Until manufacturing changes could be made, Apple suggested that
customers lift the front of the computer six inches off
the desktop and let it drop with the hope that the
chips would reseat themselves.

Another problem was that Jobs had designed the
case before the engineers finished laying out the electronic components. The circuitry would not fit into the
case, but Jobs insisted engineers make the adjust-
ment to the circuit boards rather than change his
design. As a result, some of the connectors between
the circuit boards began corroding, causing the
Apple III to stop working. The company eventually took
a $60 million loss on the Apple III and quietly removed
it from the product list in September 1985.

After his failure with the Apple III, Steve Jobs
was not invited to be involved with either the Lisa or
the Macintosh teams. He was the vice chairman of the
corporation because he was a founder, but officially
he had no title. He still made daily inspections of the
company and kept in touch with employees. First he
took an interest in the Lisa, thinking it would be the
computer for the business world. However, it was
becoming too expensive because of the point-and-
click technology Jobs had picked up from Xerox. He
looked around for another project.

Managed by Jef Raskin, the Macintosh project
was a low-priority, experimental computer, nick-
named Mac. No plans were made for its mass
production and sale. Raskin thought he was designing an inexpensive household computer, but Jobs
foresaw the future of the Macintosh. He saw that

by refining the mouse-activated point-and-click technology, the Mac could be an innovative machine that people would want. It was simple yet impressive, easy to use but on the cutting edge of computer technology. Jobs had no idea that the Macintosh and the Lisa would be competitors, which meant the sales of both computers would suffer.

Steve Jobs took over the Macintosh project and demoted Jef Raskin (employee number 31). Raskin was not happy about being replaced, but he knew that with one of the founders at the head, Apple would be more likely to put money into the Mac's development. Jobs would be managing the hardware side while Raskin stayed in charge of software and

By 1981, Apple was advertising its product as "the personal computer." Visionary Steve Jobs had dreamed of a future in which every home would have a computer—and he was helping that dream come true.

documentation. Jobs got the money and changed the Macintosh project in ways Raskin could never have imagined.

First Jobs moved the Mac project to a new location and hired two dozen employees. He thought that with an increased workforce, the Mac computer could beat the Lisa to market even though the Lisa had a two-year head start. He was so sure that he bet the Lisa project manager $5,000.

All of Steve Jobs's energy was devoted to the Macintosh computer. He had briefly considered changing the name to Bicycle, but too many people were already attached to the Macintosh name. Before the computer went to market, however, Jobs had to fight for the right to use the Macintosh trademark. The name was phonetically the same as that of McIntosh Laboratory, a manufacturer of audio equipment, so Jobs could not use the name unless McIntosh Laboratory gave its permission. Apple briefly considered shortening the name to MAC, which would stand for "mouse-activated computer," but in March 1983 the two companies signed an undisclosed agreement. Apple could use the name Macintosh but would first pay McIntosh Laboratory a sum that some say was significantly higher than $100,000.[3]

In 1980, even before the company went public, Steve Jobs started lecturing at colleges. Sometimes he spoke to full auditoriums, but what he liked best was talking to a few of the best and the brightest in an informal setting. They were able to share information, to communicate in the most technological terms, and to feel as though they were changing the world. Jobs

Jobs liked giving lectures and talking with students on college campuses across the country.

took these lectures as opportunities to recruit more people for Apple.[4]

Jobs usually sat in on interviews with new engineers and management-level employees. He sometimes sat back in his chair and put his bare feet on the table. He would ask some off-the-wall questions, such as "What kind of pizza do you like?" which took applicants by surprise—but many felt fortunate to be in the world of Steve Jobs and Apple, and they usually answered.

Meanwhile, a disappointed Raskin wrote to Apple president Michael Scott with eleven complaints about the new Mac leader. He said that Jobs missed appointments, used bad judgment, interrupted people when they talked, and did not listen to suggestions. These were all legitimate complaints. Scott himself had experienced most of them during his interactions with Jobs, but the president heard none of these negative statements from the rest of the Mac team. Although Raskin was upset with Jobs's takeover of Macintosh, Scott was delighted that Jobs was off the Lisa project, so he did not respond to the complaints.

Macintosh employees were handpicked by Jobs. They knew how he operated. They knew that he missed appointments and interrupted people. They also knew a good computer would likely be the result of their work. Jobs had a work ethic they admired. He knew what he wanted, and he and his staff worked hard until he was satisfied.

Jobs strove to staff the Macintosh team with the best and brightest. Some people from the Lisa team asked to transfer. They, like Jobs, were unhappy with the committee-style operation. Since Jobs left, the level of excellence had declined. Jobs asked an Apple II engineer if he wanted to work on Mac. The fellow said, "Yes, I guess . . . I've got some things I need to finish. It'll take me a few weeks."[5] At that point, Jobs unplugged the man's computer, put the disk drives and joystick on top, and carried it to his car. The engineer and his computer had started working for Macintosh as soon as Jobs heard the word yes.

Jobs's vision for the Macintosh was revolutionary: It should be no bigger than a phone sitting on a phone book; it would use a mouse to access programs; it would be built in the most advanced assembly plant in the world, put together by robotic assembly like those he had seen in Japan. His team was enthusiastic about breaking new ground and rose to the challenge.

Jobs pampered his team with perks. All flew first class when on company business. A stereo with six-foot-high speakers blared music for the workers. On display in the entrance were a grand piano that Jobs encouraged people to play and his BMW motorcycle that no one could ride. A masseur was on call for anyone working late. Fruit, carrot juice, and mineral water were stocked in a refrigerator for anyone, anytime. Jobs leased expensive cars for the Mac employees and had lunches and dinners catered during meetings. And, so that each person would feel he or she had contributed individually to the project, the signatures of the team members were etched into the inside of each case for the first few years of production. Jobs had reestablished the personal, self-motivated organization of Apple's roots. Chris Espinosa, then twenty-two, described the Mac team as being "like an endless cocktail party, with chips and software instead of drinks."[6]

The Mac team called themselves pirates. The flag they flew outside their new building was the skull and crossbones with an apple for the eye. Their name and reputation were a result of pirating excellent employees from other companies and divisions of Apple, and pirating the mouse activation system from Xerox.

Scott and Jobs continued to disagree on most aspects of Apple operations. By 1981 Scott had been president for four years and had personal problems

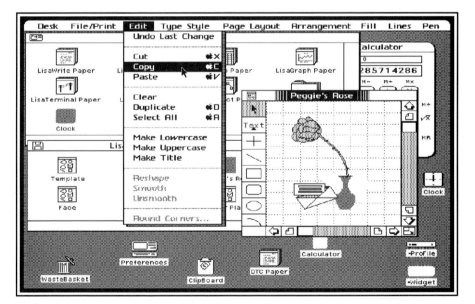

The Lisa featured pull-down menus and a point-and-click operating system. The graphical user interface (GUI, pronounced "gooey") introduced in the Lisa and the Macintosh made computers much more user-friendly.

that interfered with his effectiveness. While he was on a long weekend in Hawaii, Apple's executive staff voted to ask for his resignation as president. This resulted in the shifting of the top three positions at Apple. Markkula assumed Scott's duties as president while Jobs took Markkula's place as chairman of the board. Scott was left with Jobs's title of vice chairman, a position without power. With little experience in technology and management, Steve Jobs at twenty-six became the chairman of a $2 billion corporation.

In February 1982 Steve Jobs started hosting retreats, a tradition that would unite and motivate the Mac team. A bus would leave Apple in the morning, meetings would be held in the afternoon, and a guest speaker would make a presentation at dinner. Each group would summarize the work it had accomplished and its goals. Then Jobs would present his synopsis of what he understood and lead a discussion. For the first retreat, Jobs had T-shirts made with the date May 16, 1983, printed on it. This was the date of the National Computer Conference in Anaheim, California, and the projected introduction date of the Macintosh. This date was only fifteen months away, and the team had a lot of work to do.

IBM—Big Blue, as its competition called it—entered the personal computer market in August 1982. Steve Jobs welcomed IBM in a full advertisement, complimenting the company on its first personal computer. Jobs and others believed IBM would suffer the same start-up problems that Apple had. They did not take the competition seriously. In fact, the Mac division bought an IBM and took it apart. Relieved to find it

Jobs bought an apartment in the San Remo to use whenever he is in New York City. This beautiful building overlooks both Central Park and the Hudson River.

crude and unwieldy, they reported that it was large and clumsy compared to the Apple and introduced no new technology.[7] IBM, however, had a long track record of satisfying customers and was able to adapt quickly by sending thousands of representatives into the field to find out what customers wanted on the PC. Within two years IBM had surpassed Apple in total dollar sales, and Apple's percentage in the computer market began to shrink dramatically.

Out on a Limb

After Apple went public, Steve Jobs, the charismatic founder, became a worldwide celebrity. Magazines featured his picture on their covers and wrote articles about his fast-growing company. Jobs was on the cover of *Time* in February 1982 and on the cover of *Life* the following month.

At the end of 1982, *Time* published its traditional end-of-the-year issue. Instead of "Man of the Year," *Time* named the personal computer "Machine of the Year," saying the computer had changed the lives of so many people. Millions of people were disappointed with the announcement, but Steve Jobs was probably the most disappointed.[1]

Time had intended to present Steve Jobs as "Man of the Year," but the reporter who interviewed Jobs wrote a critical feature article containing many negative comments about Jobs. The editors of the newsmagazine decided that since the article was uncomplimentary, they would designate the computer as "Machine of the Year."[2] It seemed a double standard that *Time* celebrated the computer but criticized the visionary who intended to put a machine in every home, office, and classroom. No other individual was featured in that issue either in a positive or a negative way. But, then, no other individual had been interviewed.

Much of what the article said was true, but it was without balance. It did not mention how compassionate Jobs could be. When an engineer was hospitalized because of cancer, Steve Jobs paid for a private room, paid all medical bills, visited him every day, and made sure he had all that he wanted and needed, including a private nurse. The article failed to say that at parties, Jobs would be at the computer with children, showing them the endless possibilities of these machines. It also failed to inform readers that Jobs was lobbying the state government to get more nutritious food in the schools. No mention was made of the contributions Jobs made to the organization that aided the blind people of Nepal. Steve Jobs had also put nine thousand Apple II computers in California secondary schools and was working on a program to put computers in prisons for inmates' education.

At one of the concerts to earn money for the prison program, Jobs met Joan Baez, a popular folksinger of the 1960s and 1970s. He was intrigued by her, even though she was fifteen years older than he was. At twenty-seven, Jobs had developed a desire for a settled life and children. Friends were surprised when he mentioned at dinner one evening, "If only she were of child-bearing age, I'd marry her."[3] Although Jobs and Baez did not marry, they remained friends. Baez appeared at many Mac parties throughout 1982 and 1983.

The Macintosh team had a few romances and a few divorces. In general, though, people had little time for socialization of any sort. They went to dinner as a group, often for pizza, sometimes to a Mexican restaurant. They had to eat somewhere that could provide a vegetarian meal for Jobs. A fellow diner always paid for Jobs's meal because he never carried cash. One night while eating refried beans, Jobs bragged to his teammates that he had not eaten meat for many years. One friend remarked that refried beans were made with animal fat. Jobs refused to believe it and asked the waitress, who confirmed the report. Jobs insisted on seeing the kitchen, where he observed chefs frying the beans in animal fat. He dropped refried beans from the list of foods he would eat.

Steve Jobs turned twenty-eight on February 24, 1983, and the Mac team had a great surprise for him. They rented a billboard for the day along the route that Jobs took to work. It said, "Happy 28th Steve. The Journey is the Reward. The Pirates."[4] Unfortunately, Jobs never saw the message. He stayed home with a cold that day.

That year Apple finally hired a new president, John Sculley. Before he was offered the position, the

Apple board of directors decided that Sculley and Jobs should get to know each other. Whenever Jobs was at his apartment in New York City, he met with Sculley, who was chief executive officer (CEO) of Pepsi-Cola. They took long walks in Central Park, they ate together, and they became friends before they had to be working companions. Everyone had to be convinced that the relationship of the new president and the chairman would be beneficial to Apple. Sculley was indecisive about accepting the offer, so Jobs finally asked the Pepsi executive if he would rather make sugared water or change the world. Sculley decided he would like a chance at changing the world.

The Mac team remained essentially unchanged when Sculley reorganized Apple in early 1983. Jobs kept control of the Macintosh division, and everything went fine between him and the new president until later in the year when Sculley decided to merge Lisa and Macintosh. Apple stock had plummeted from $63 a share to $21 a share, due mostly to the failure of Lisa to become a successfully selling computer. Combining the two teams would save money. Jobs would retain the title of manager.

Apple planned a big advertising budget to introduce the Macintosh. The first nationwide commercial was aired during the televised Super Bowl game on January 22, 1984. The Regis McKenna Public Relations Agency leaked that Apple was airing a commercial like no other in the history of advertising. The commercial, created by the Chiat/Day advertising agency, cost $800,000 to produce, reached 50 percent

Apple president John Sculley, right, with Steve Jobs in Central Park in New York City. The bag on the bench holds a Macintosh computer.

of the nation's men and 36 percent of the women, and became one of the most remembered commercials in history.[5]

The *1984*, or "Big Brother," commercial featured two hundred bald-headed people in nondescript clothing staring glassy-eyed at an enormous television screen. As the face on the screen (Big Brother) talked about information purification, a woman in red shorts ran down the aisle swinging a sledgehammer. Just before a force of policemen could stop her, she swung the sledgehammer into the screen, smashing the image and silencing Big Brother. Making a reference to George Orwell's novel *1984*, which characterizes an authoritarian government as "Big Brother," a notice at the end read, "On January 24th, Apple Computer will introduce Macintosh. And you'll see why 1984 won't be like '1984.'"[6]

The entire commercial was shown officially only twice, once on December 15, 1983, at 1:00 A.M. in Twin Falls, Idaho, so that it could be considered for the 1983 advertising awards and again during the Super Bowl. Immediately following the Super Bowl, all three major networks replayed it during their evening news shows, and hundreds of newspapers and magazines wrote about it. Since then it has been replayed numerous times as an example of noteworthy advertising, as well as during media programs featuring the Apple Computer Company.

The Macintosh was introduced to the public two days after the Super Bowl, during Apple's annual shareholders' meeting. During the meeting Jobs described how he had reverted to a small-business attitude while developing the Mac. "I just decided that I was going to go off and do that myself with a small group. Sort of go back to the garage, to design the Macintosh. They didn't take us very seriously. I think Scotty [Michael Scott, then president of Apple] was just sort of humoring me."[7] He did not mention that the project took nearly a year longer than anticipated.

The actual unveiling of the Macintosh was a spectacle. The first five rows of the packed auditorium held the Mac team wearing identical Macintosh T-shirts. Other Apple employees stood in a nearby room, watching the televised proceedings. The theme song from *Chariots of Fire*, a movie about the success of an underdog, prepared the audience. Jobs read a few lines from Bob Dylan's song "The Times They Are a-Changin'," and the business portion of the meeting commenced.

Then Steve Jobs came back with the Macintosh computer, which gave a little speech in a computer-generated voice, introducing "the man who's been like a father to me, Steve Jobs."[8] The auditorium erupted with applause, shouts, and a standing ovation. The introduction of the Macintosh was a huge success.

Only the members of the Macintosh team knew that most of them had not slept during the past seven days. A week before the Mac's debut, the software was still not finished. It looked like an impossible task, but Jobs told them how good they were and that he knew they could do it. The pep talk kept them awake for a week while they finished the programs. The final copy of the software was handed to Jobs just fifteen minutes before the deadline.[9]

Jobs and the Mac team were thrilled by the Macintosh hoopla. Sales took off, and Jobs was sure they would meet his projection of 5 million sales in the first two years. But sales slowed after a couple of months, and only two hundred thousand Macs had been sold by November 1984.

The Macintosh did not have everything people wanted. Instead of surveying the public as IBM had, Jobs planned the computer that he personally would want. The Mac had state-of-the-art graphics capability. Jean Yates of Yates Ventures said, "The Mac will go down in history as *the* box that made it possible to put graphics in general business correspondence."[10] But the Mac also had a small screen, no color, few programs, and no printer. Worst of all, it was not IBM-compatible.

In May 1985 the two-year relationship between Jobs and Sculley began to deteriorate. Apple was not earning money as projected. Although the Apple II was still being manufactured at a profit, neither the Lisa nor the Macintosh was selling well. Sculley decided another reorganization was necessary, and the first to be targeted was Steve Jobs, head of the Lisa/Mac division. Sculley thought someone else could do a better job uniting the two teams.

Jobs's new assignment was to be in charge of new products. Unhappy with this change, Jobs tried to turn things around. While Sculley was on vacation, Jobs attempted to get him fired. As chairman, Jobs gathered the board together to vote Sculley out of office, but not enough board members agreed.

Upon his return, Sculley heard about the failed

coup and decided to resign, but his friends persuaded him not to. Instead, Sculley went to the board and got enough members to vote to remove Jobs. On May 31, 1985, Steve Jobs was relieved of all operational positions at Apple Computer.

The world found out about Jobs's demotion on Sunday morning, June 1. Jobs stayed in his house that day playing Bob Dylan records, including his favorite, "The Times They Are a-Changin'." His phone rang continuously, but he did not answer. A few close friends, including his girlfriend at that time, kept him company through the day and then left him alone with his thoughts.

Jobs eventually told Sculley that he was willing to accept the position in the new products division, but Sculley withdrew his offer, saying, "There is no place for you in my Apple."[11]

Jobs reported the feeling it gave him: "You've probably had somebody punch you in the stomach and it knocks the wind out of you and you can't breathe."[12]

Jobs's role at Apple Computer has changed a number of times.

Family, Films, and Fresh Starts

As of June 1, 1985, Steve Jobs no longer had operational responsibilities at Apple Computer Company. He retained the title of chairman of the board and was put in charge of "global thinking." He was given an office far from headquarters. The Apple employees called it Siberia. Jobs had little to do except think.

Wherever he was, Jobs thought about his past and his future. He even thought about entering politics, but he belonged to neither major political party and had, in fact, never voted.[1] He talked to people he liked and respected at Apple, and on September 12, 1985, he talked to the Apple board of directors about a new plan he had come up with.

Steve Jobs told the board that he and a few

"low-level" employees from Apple planned to start a new company. Their goal was to make computers that met the needs of colleges and would not compete with the current Apple market. The board seemed interested in Jobs's plan and even suggested that Apple invest in his company. They asked for more information.

The next day, Friday the thirteenth, Jobs gave Sculley a list of the five Apple employees he wanted for his new company. Sculley and the board were furious. These were not low-level employees. They were people who knew the secrets of the Apple computers. The board of directors was outraged and discussed removing Jobs as chairman of the board and starting legal action against him.[2] But Jobs made the decision first, and on September 17 he resigned from all responsibilities at Apple.

Jobs did not go quietly. Not only did he send a letter of resignation to Markkula, he sent press releases to all the papers, thinking he would get the public's sympathy. Just the opposite happened. Apple stock rose a full point that day, indicating that the public no longer revered Steve Jobs.

Six days later Jobs received notice that Apple had filed a lawsuit against him. He could not use any of his knowledge of Apple computers to design his new computer systems. This was contradictory: On May 31, Apple executives had told him that he was an incompetent manager with little knowledge or technical skill. Now they were claiming he was a major threat.[3] He could not be both incompetent and a threat. In January 1986, the lawsuit was settled out of court. Jobs could take the five people he had selected, but he could not hire additional Apple employees for six months. Apple also insisted that any computers Jobs's new company made must be more powerful than any Apple computer. This would eliminate competition between the companies.

At thirty, Steve Jobs was starting from scratch for the third time. He had been successful first with the startup of Apple and then with the Macintosh. He was confident that he could do it again.[4]

Jobs needed money to start his new computer company, so by February 1986 he had sold all but one share of his Apple stock. He said he kept only one share so that he would still receive Apple's annual reports. He now had $135 million to invest in new projects.

At the same time a very different kind of business got Steve Jobs's attention. He invested $10 million to become the major shareholder and chairman of the board of Pixar Animation Studios. Pixar was the computer division of Lucasfilm, Ltd., the company that had made possible the *Star Wars* and *Jurassic Park* movies. Pixar's $120,000 computer could process three-dimensional graphics at a speed of 40 million instructions per second.

Jobs thought Pixar had a future; it just needed money. Disney agreed to release three Pixar movies: *Toy Story* and two others. Jobs contributed $50 million of his personal money. He said later that if he had known it would take that much money, he probably would not have bought the company. As it was, the money was spent a little at a time, and he never personally kept track. After four years in the making, *Toy Story* was released on November 22, 1995, and earned more than $189 million for Pixar.

The two other films released by Pixar and Disney, *A Bug's Life* (1998) and *Toy Story 2* (1999), were equally successful. When Pixar went public about the same time *Toy Story* appeared, the company's estimated worth was $710 million, and Jobs owned 80 percent of it. But Pixar was like a hobby to Jobs. He was interested in what was going on, he gave Pixar money when it was needed, but he let the decisions be made by qualified people.

Meanwhile, determined to build a better computer, Jobs formed NeXT Computer, Inc. The company originally started up in Jobs's house, just as the Apple I had a decade earlier. Senior staff members would go looking for office space during the day, then sneak Jobs in during the night so landlords would not recognize him and raise the lease rates. One possible building was an abandoned monastery—ironic since Jobs had once thought of joining a monastery. They decided on a small office building in the Stanford hills surrounded by scenic open land where Jobs could spend hours walking, as he had in the past with John Sculley.[5]

This time Jobs asked his customers what they wanted. He talked to college professors and students and designed the NeXT computer around their needs. He invested $7 million of his money in NeXT, but he needed much more. Billionaire H. Ross Perot called Jobs the day after being impressed by a television documentary about NeXT. Before he hung up, Perot said, "If you ever need an investor, call me."[6]

Jobs waited a week before inviting Perot to come look at his firm and meet its employees. In November 1986, Jobs received $20 million from Perot in exchange for 16 percent of NeXT. Perot said that he was investing in quality.

Jobs unveiled the new computer in October 1988. The twelve-inch cube with a unique black matte finish drew a great deal of interest. The press predicted excellent sales. But the public had to wait eleven months before it would be available.

In June 1989, three months before the NeXT computer became available, a Japanese company paid $100 million for another 16 percent of NeXT. Jobs's new company now had a value of $600 million. Jobs held 46 percent of the shares. He was once again among the richest men in the world.

The NeXT computer failed to deliver what educators had asked for. It was too expensive to be a personal computer and too underpowered to be a workstation. The marketing team took advantage of the computer's shortcomings by inventing the term "personal workstation" and targeting the business community as well as colleges.

For thirty-six-year-old Steve Jobs, both his business and personal life were running smoothly. On March 18, 1991, he married Laurene Powell at the Ahwahnee Hotel in Yosemite National Park. The twenty-seven-year-old bride had been a graduate student studying business administration when Jobs met her during a talk he was giving at Stanford

Jobs talked to college professors and students before designing the NeXT computer.

University. After the wedding she moved into the almost empty Woodside mansion. Their son, Reed Paul, named for the college Jobs once attended, was born at the end of the year.

In the middle of 1991, NeXT suffered several setbacks. One of the founders quit. Then one of the major retail chains that sold NeXT computers went bankrupt. Finally, H. Ross Perot resigned from the board of directors in response to inefficiencies he saw in the company. He told Jobs, "I shouldn't have let you guys have all that money. Biggest mistake I made."[7]

The NeXT computer did not sell well because it was priced too high for college students, did not have a color display, and used a nonstandard disk drive. But the software created by NeXT was superior and deserved to find a market of its own. On February 10, 1993, the day later referred to as Black Tuesday, Jobs laid off more than half of his 530 employees and announced that the NeXT hardware division would be sold to Japanese investors, and the company's focus would be on selling its software.

The software never became popular, but NeXT's Internet development tool, called WebObjects, was so successful that Jobs and his friend Laurence J. Ellison considered using their profits to buy out Apple. They thought they could turn the company around. Together they were worth more than $5 billion, but they were unable to agree on how to finance the buyout.

A survey by a major investment organization named Apple Computer the worst-run company of 1996. Apple had fired four presidents by February of that year and desperately needed something and someone to revitalize the company. Their solution was to purchase the NeXT software company from Steve Jobs and hire Jobs as an adviser to Apple. Jobs said, "I still have very deep feelings for Apple, and it gives me great joy to play a role in architecting Apple's future."[8]

For almost two years Jobs acted as an adviser to Apple. When not at work he was enjoying life with Laurene, son Reed, and daughter Erin Sienna, born in 1995. Lisa, Chris-Ann's daughter, had also become part of her father's life, and by 1996, when she entered Harvard University, she was a frequent participant in family activities. (Another daughter, Eve, was born in 1998.)

In 1997 the Jobs family visited a resort in Hawaii. Six-year-old Reed had many activities to keep him busy during the day. He won a fishing contest, but he was not allowed to collect the prize—a bag of candy—because his father thought candy and ice cream were not healthy. Instead, his father took him to the gift shop to pick out a souvenir. Another time during the vacation, Reed was scared by rough water during a whale watching trip. Jobs asked the captain to return to shore. When he refused, Jobs considered his son's condition and called for a rescue boat to come get them.[9]

Jobs still enjoyed his association with Pixar. In fact, when asked if he would take over as CEO (chief executive officer) of Apple, Jobs responded, "I've already got the best job in the world, which is to be part of the team at Pixar."[10]

In 1997, Jobs's sister Mona Simpson published

"I've got the best job in the world," said Jobs, "which is to be part of the team at Pixar." With his movie connection, Jobs again found his face splashed across magazine covers.

her third novel, *A Regular Guy*. The main character shares many characteristics and experiences with Steve Jobs. Was her story really about Steve? "There is some biographical truth in what I do," said Mona, "but I want the license to make things up—which I do."[11]

During the summer of 1997, it became clear to the world that Steve Jobs had been more than just an adviser to Apple. He had no official authority but was making major decisions, the kind of decisions a CEO would make. He had been running product review meetings and had presided over meetings to improve Apple's sales strategy. He had even replaced the food service company running the Apple cafeteria.

In July 1997 Steve Jobs turned down offers to become the CEO and chairman of the board of Apple, but he did agree to become a board member. Now he had an official link to the company, and people started considering him to be Apple's unofficial leader.

A month later Steve Jobs delivered the keynote address at the Macworld Expo in Boston. He was greeted with a standing ovation and shouts of "Steve! Steve!"[12] He proceeded to make two shocking announcements. First, three of the five board members had resigned, including Mike Markkula, who in 1976 had promised four years of leadership but had given twenty. The second disclosure initially had some observers outraged. Jobs announced an alliance with Microsoft that he was sure would benefit both companies. The same people who had shouted "Steve! Steve!" now shouted "No! No!"[13]

Jobs reported that Microsoft would invest

$150 million in Apple in exchange for Apple's preloading Microsoft's Internet Explorer in every Mac. Jobs said, "We have to let go of the notion that for Apple to win, Microsoft has to lose. For Apple to win, Apple has to do a really good job."[14] By the end of the speech, most of the audience agreed. The public was delighted and Apple stock rose 33 percent that day.

Shortly after the Macworld Expo, Steve Jobs had an idea for a new and different ad campaign. He rehired Chiat/Day, the advertising agency that had developed the unforgettable *1984* commercial for the Super Bowl. "Think Different" was the phrase Jobs wanted as the center of this campaign, and he personally made calls to secure rights to some of his favorite photographs.[15] Using personalities such as Albert Einstein, Alfred Hitchcock, and Amelia Earhart, he wanted to demonstrate that people whose thinking was different from the majority could change the world—and companies could think different, too.

With Jobs's "think different" attitude, Apple's business kept improving. At the Macworld Expo in San Francisco in January 1998, a bearded Steve Jobs, dressed in a black leather jacket, black long-sleeved shirt, and faded jeans, announced that the company would be making a profit for the first time in two years. A $45 million profit was projected for the first quarter. Employees and stockholders were overjoyed.

Then in May Jobs surprised the computer world during a media event he arranged at De Anza College in Cupertino. Clean-shaven and dressed in a suit, Jobs told the reporters and businesspeople in the auditorium that Apple had refined its manufacturing focus to concentrate on only four computers: a desktop and a portable professional model, and a desktop and a portable consumer model. The professional models were already for sale, and the consumer portable would be out the following year.

Observers knew the new consumer desktop was beneath the veil on stage. When Steve Jobs pulled the fabric away and introduced the iMac, everyone gasped. The new Apple was teal blue and white, shaped like a cone, and glowed in the dark. On the screen was the message "Hello again." The iMac, meaning "internet Mac," began shipping in August 1998 and sold briskly. Consumers were so taken with the machine and its fruit colors that one iMac sold every fifteen seconds of every day for the next year.

Since 1995 when Jobs returned to Apple as an adviser, the media had asked over and over how long he had planned to stay with the company. He had refused offers to become permanent CEO of Apple several times and was irritated that the media kept asking. Finally, in an interview with *Business Week* in mid-1998, he said, "I'm Apple's interim CEO, and it won't be forever, and I'm doing the best that I can."[16] He wanted only $1 a year for his work so that he could be on the company health plan.

Jobs had slashed Apple's expenses by cutting back on the number of research projects, eliminating three-fourths of the company's suppliers, and decreasing the inventory from several months' worth of merchandise to less than a day's worth. The remaining suppliers agreed to give Apple a larger

"Hello, again," read the computer screen. Consumers flocked to the stores to buy Apple Computer's fruit-colored iMAC.

discount, and storage expenses were cut dramatically. He also severed Apple's business relationship with companies making Apple computer clones.

Research into a few key new products continued, and on July 20, 1999, Jobs unveiled the fourth Apple Computer: the anticipated iBook, a laptop computer that needed no wires to connect to the Internet. Its edges were rounded, it had a carrying handle, and it came in two colors: tangerine and blueberry.

By January 2000, Apple was a $6.1 billion company. Sales had increased from 3 percent of the computer market to 6 percent. Steve Jobs finally agreed to be the official CEO of Apple. When Jobs had taken the helm as "interim CEO" in July 1997, Apple Computer stock was down to about $13 per share. After Jobs revamped the company, the stock was worth more than $100 per share.[17]

Visions of the Artist

Throughout Steve Jobs's career he has been referred to as a visionary, a person who can envison unknown or future things. John McCollum, Jobs's high school electronics teacher, said that Jobs had a different way of looking at things. Apple's president John Sculley told Jobs to do what he did best—to be in charge of new products. Steve Jobs not only imagined and dreamed of changing the world, he looked into the future and in the process changed the world.

Apple had been making computers for nine years when, in a 1985 magazine interview, Jobs said, "The primary reasons to buy a computer for your home now are that you want to do some business work at home or you want to run educational software for yourself or

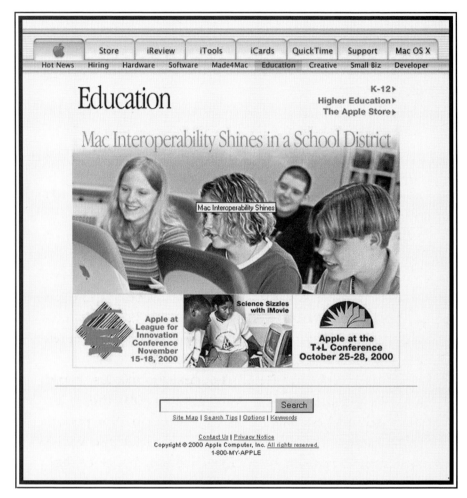

"*We started out to get a computer in the hands of everyday people, and we succeeded beyond our wildest dreams*," said Jobs.

your children."[1] Computer word-processing programs were difficult to use, so most people continued using typewriters for letters and reports. Also, elaborate drawing programs were unimaginable. People did not *need* personal computers in 1985. They *wanted* them because computers were new and exciting machines.

Being a visionary, Steve Jobs foresaw a need. He said, "The most compelling reason for most people to buy a computer for the home will be to link it into a nationwide communications network."[2] This network, now called the Internet, assists people all over the world in many areas of their life, including travel, medicine, research, entertainment, and literature. Only a visionary could have predicted such a revolution.

He also foresaw computers' ability to follow the stock market, and he knew computers would be writing letters or reports based on data analysis. He anticipated double-sided disk drives, hard disks, and sophisticated software years before they became reality.

In 2000 Jobs predicted that desktop movies would be bigger than desktop publishing.[3] In 2001 the iBook was equipped with a DVD-ROM drive so that people could watch movies, too. It could also let you make your own movies from a digital camcorder. Jobs had made his prediction come true.

Few people begin their professional career as vice chairman of a company. It usually takes education and experience to achieve such a position. Jobs had neither. He learned informally, from on-the-job training. He has studied the industry since Hewlett-Packard

Visionary Steve Jobs continues to stun consumers with new products like the iBook, upper right, and the G4, a computer that fits into an eight-inch cube.

demonstrated a computer for the Explorer Club when he was a youngster, and he continues to learn. He has gained respect and admiration from many who thought him incapable or immature in his early days at Apple.

His return as CEO fulfilled another prediction Jobs had made to Sheff in 1985. He said, "I hope that throughout my life . . . the thread of my life and the thread of Apple weave in and out of each other, like a tapestry. There may be a few years when I'm not there, but I'll always come back."[4]

Many of Steve Jobs's innovations came together at the July 2000 Macworld Expo when he unveiled Apple's newest computer, the eight-inch cube called the G4. It had no fan but was cooled by convection through a ventilation channel. Most surfaces were smooth; no buttons stuck out and the single slot was camouflaged in the top. Even the mouse had no buttons. He reported, "We make progress by eliminating things, by removing the superfluous."[5] It was obviously Steve Jobs's computer. It was his vision and the work of an artist.

In 1991 Apple's distinguished employee Guy Kawasaki said, "Medicine will cure death and government will repeal taxes before Steve will fail."[6] Many might say he had failed here and there along the way, but any major accomplishment is bound to have setbacks. Steve Jobs is successful because he is a visionary, he keeps learning from his mistakes, and he is persistent.

Only Steve Jobs knows what visions fill his mind. The world will wonder until the veil is lifted and the artist reveals his next work.

1955—Steven Paul Jobs, born February 24 in San Francisco, California, is adopted by Paul and Clara Jobs.

1957—Steve's sister, Patty, joins the family.

1968—Steve Jobs meets Steve Wozniak.

1972—Jobs graduates from Homestead High School, Los Altos, California, and attends one semester at Reed College in Portland, Oregon.

1975—Spends several months traveling around India.

1976—Joins with Wozniak to build and market a tabletop computer. Apple Computer Company is formed April 1.

1977—Partners sign incorporation papers for Apple on January 3; the Apple II, the first mass-marketed personal computer, is introduced in April; Michael M. Scott is hired as president of Apple in May.

1980—Jobs is removed from managerial role at Apple but stays on as vice chairman. Apple goes public December 12; the Apple III is shipped.

1981—Jobs becomes chairman of the board of Apple.

1982—Jobs discovers he has a biological sister, Mona Simpson.

1983—Apple introduces the Lisa, a computer controlled by a mouse.

1984—Jobs unveils the Macintosh computer.

1985—Jobs is awarded the National Technology Medal by President Ronald Reagan; after a power struggle with Apple's president, Jobs resigns; forms NeXT Computer, Inc.

1986—With money from the sale of his Apple stock, Jobs buys into Pixar Animation Studios.

1987—Receives the Jefferson Award for Public Service, which is given by the American Institute of Public Service.

1989—Is named Entrepreneur of the Decade by *Inc.* magazine.

1991—Marries Laurene Powell.

1993—Lays off more than half of NeXT employees and announces sale of NeXT hardware to Japanese investors.

1996—Sells NeXT software division to Apple and becomes a nonsalaried adviser to Apple.

1997—Negotiates a deal with Microsoft and agrees to serve as interim CEO of Apple.

1998—Jobs unveils the iMac.

1999—The iBook is introduced.

2000—Jobs becomes Apple's CEO and unveils the G4 Cube.

Chapter 1. Mission Nearly Impossible

1. Jeffrey S. Young, *Steve Jobs: The Journey Is the Reward* (Glenview, Ill.: Scott, Foresman and Co., 1988), p. 93.

2. Everett M. Rogers and Judith K. Larson, *Silicon Valley Fever: Growth of High-Technology Culture* (New York: Basic Books, Inc., 1984), p. 9.

3. Michael S. Malone, *Infinite Loop: How the World's Most Insanely Great Computer Company Went Insane* (New York: Doubleday, 1999), p. 78.

4. Jim Carlton, *Apple: The Inside Story of Intrigue, Egomania, and Business Blunders* (New York: Harper Business, 1997), p. 10.

5. Owen W. Linzmayer, *Apple Confidential: The Real Story of Apple Computer, Inc.* (San Francisco: No Starch Press, 1999), p. 3.

6. Michael Moritz, *The Little Kingdom: The Private Story of Apple Computer* (New York: William Morrow, 1984), p. 144.

7. Young, p. 97.

Chapter 2. Brilliance by Bribery

1. Michael Moritz, *The Little Kingdom: The Private Story of Apple Computer* (New York: William Morrow, 1984), p. 39.

2. David Sheff, "Playboy Interview: Steven Jobs," *Playboy*, February 1985, p. 176.

3. Moritz, p. 39.

4. Jeffrey S. Young, *Steve Jobs: The Journey Is the Reward* (Glenview, Ill.: Scott, Foresman and Co., 1988), p. 23.

5. Ibid., pp. 23–24.

6. Paul Freiberger and Michael Swaine, *Fire in the Valley: The Making of the Personal Computer* (Berkeley, Calif.: Osborne/McGraw-Hill, 1984), p. 206.

7. Moritz, p. 39.

8. Young, p. 40.

Chapter 3. Experiments and Electronics

1. David Sheff, "Playboy Interview: Steven Jobs," February 1985, p. 176.

2. Michael Moritz, *The Little Kingdom: The Private Story of Apple Computer* (New York: William Morrow, 1984), p. 55.

3. Ibid., p. 42.

4. Ibid., p. 43.

5. Ibid., p. 64.

6. Jeffrey S. Young, *Steve Jobs: The Journey Is the Reward* (Glenview, Ill.: Scott, Foresman and Co., 1988), pp. 32–33.

7. Moritz, p. 64.

8. Young, p. 38.

9. Moritz, p. 66.

10. Sheff, p. 176.

11. Young, p. 40.

12. Paul Freiberger and Michael Swaine, *Fire in the Valley: The Making of the Personal Computer* (Berkeley, Calif.: Osborne/McGraw-Hill, 1984), p. 208.

13. Moritz, p. 71.

14. Ibid., p. 73.

15. Ibid., pp. 77–78.

16. Ibid., p. 74.

Chapter 4. Free Spirit

1. Michael Moritz, *The Little Kingdom: The Private Story of Apple Computer* (New York: William Morrow, 1984), p. 87.

2. Ibid., p. 88.

3. Lee Butcher, *Accidental Millionaire: The Rise and Fall of Steve Jobs at Apple Computer* (New York: Paragon House, 1988), p. 43.

4. Moritz, p. 91.

5. Ibid., p. 90.

6. Frank Rose, *West of Eden: The End of Innocence at Apple Computer* (New York: Viking, 1989), p. 28.

7. Jeffrey S. Young, *Steve Jobs: The Journey Is the Reward* (Glenview, Ill.: Scott, Foresman and Co., 1988), p. 57.

8. David Sheff, "Playboy Interview: Steven Jobs," *Playboy*, February, 1985, p. 178.

9. Moritz, p. 93.

10. Butcher, p. 49.

11. Sheff, p. 178.

Chapter 5. India, Insights, and Inventions

1. David Sheff, "Playboy Interview: Steven Jobs," *Playboy*, February 1985, p. 178.

2. Paul Freiberger and Michael Swaine, *Fire in the Valley: The Making of the Personal Computer* (Berkeley, Calif., Osborne/McGraw-Hill, 1984), p. 209.

3. Lee Butcher, *Accidental Millionaire: The Rise and Fall of Steve Jobs at Apple Computer* (New York: Paragon House, 1988), p. 50.

4. Jeffrey S. Young, *Steve Jobs: The Journey Is the Reward* (Glenview, Ill.: Scott, Foresman and Co., 1988), pp. 67–68.

5. Ibid., p. 69.

6. Michael Moritz, *The Little Kingdom: The Private Story of Apple Computer* (New York: William Morrow, 1984), p. 99.

7. Young, p. 72.

Chapter 6. Apple: The First Byte

1. Everett M. Rogers and Judith Larsen, *Silicon Valley Fever: Growth of High-Technology Culture* (New York: Basic Books, Inc., 1984), p. 14.

2. Owen W. Linzmayer, *Apple Confidential: The Real Story of Apple Computer, Inc.* (San Francisco: No Starch Press, 1999), p. 5.

3. Michael S. Malone, *Infinite Loop: How the World's Most Insanely Great Computer Company Went Insane* (New York: Doubleday, 1999), p. 85.

4. Moritz, pp. 149–150.

5. Rogers and Larsen, p. 16.

6. Malone, p. 56.

7. Paul Freiberger and Michael Swaine, *Fire in the Valley: The Making of the Personal Computer* (Berkeley, Calif.: Osborne/McGraw-Hill, 1984), p. 215.

Chapter 7. Designs, Details, and Dinners

1. Michael Moritz, *The Little Kingdom: The Private Story of Apple Computer* (New York: William Morrow, 1984), p. 186.

2. Michael S. Malone, *Infinite Loop: How the World's Most Insanely Great Computer Company Went Insane* (New York: Doubleday, 1999), p. 134.

3. Moritz, p. 198.

4. Memo on display in the Apple Museum, Cupertino, California.

5. Owen W. Linzmayer, *Apple Confidential: The Real Story of Apple Computer* (San Francisco: No Starch Press, 1999), p. 6.

6. Moritz, p. 224.

7. Jeffrey S. Young, *Steve Jobs: The Journey Is the Reward* (Glenview, Ill.: Scott Foresman and Co., 1988), p. 127.

8. Ibid., p. 154.

9. Lee Butcher, *Accidental Millionaire: The Rise and Fall of Steve Jobs at Apple Computer* (New York: Paragon House, 1988), p. 140.

10. Young, p. 260.

11. Butcher, p. 125.

Chapter 8. Youngest of the Superrich

1. Jeffrey S. Young, *Steve Jobs: The Journey Is the Reward* (Glenview, Ill.: Scott Foresman and Co., 1988), p. 194.

2. Michael Moritz, *The Little Kingdom: The Private Story of Apple Computer* (New York: William Morrow, 1984), p. 280.

3. Owen W. Linzmayer, *Apple Confidential: The Real Story of Apple Computer, Inc.* (San Francisco: No Starch Press, 1999), p. 65.

4. Young, p. 232.

5. Ibid., p. 222.

6. Michael Rogers, "It's the Apple of His Eye," *Newsweek*, January 30, 1984, p. 55.

7. Young, p. 234.

Chapter 9. Out on a Limb

1. Jeffrey S. Young, *Steve Jobs: The Journey Is the Reward* (Glenview, Ill.: Scott, Foresman and Co., 1988), pp. 289–290.

2. David A. Kaplan, *The Silicon Boys and Their Valley of Dreams* (New York: William Morrow and Co., 1999), p. 309.

3. Ibid., p. 259.

4. Young, p. 301.

5. Owen W. Linzmayer, *Apple Confidential: The Real Story of Apple Computer, Inc.* (San Francisco: No Starch Press, 1999), p. 90.

6. Ibid., p. 87.

7. David Sheff, "Playboy Interview: Steven Jobs," *Playboy*, February 1985, p. 58.

8. Young, p. 335.

9. Ibid., p. 328.

10. Ann M. Morrison, "Apple Bites Back," *Fortune*, February 20, 1984, p. 91.

11. Young, p. 400.

12. Eric Gelman, "Showdown in Silicon Valley," *Newsweek*, September 30, 1985, p. 47.

Chapter 10. Family, Films, and Fresh Starts

1. Bro Uttal, "The Adventures of Steve Jobs (Cont'd)," *Fortune*, October 14, 1985, p. 122.

2. Ibid., p. 124.

3. Owen W. Linzmayer, *Apple Confidential: The Real Story of Apple Computer, Inc.* (San Francisco: No Starch Press, 1999), p. 126.

4. Eric Gelman, "Showdown in Silicon Valley," *Newsweek*, September 30, 1985, p. 50.

5. Alan Deutschman, *The Second Coming of Steve Jobs* (New York: Broadway Books, 2000), p. 19.

6. Linzmayer, p. 169.

7. Ibid., p. 172.

8. Jim Carlton, *Apple: The Inside Story of Intrigue, Egomania, and Business Blunders* (New York: Harper Business, 1997), p. 412.

9. Deutschman, p. 244.

10. Carlton, p. 433.

11. Deutschman, p. 225.

12. Carlton, p. 433.

13. Ibid., p. 434.

14. Ibid., p. 432.

15. Peter Burrows, "A Peek at Steve Jobs' Plan," *Business Week*, November 17, 1997, p. 146.

16. A. Reinhardt, "Steve Jobs: 'There's Sanity Returning'," *Business Week*, May 25, 1998, p. 63.

17. John Markoff, "Jobs Drops 'Interim' From Title at Apple," *The New York Times*, January 6, 2000, p. C2.

Chapter 11. Visions of the Artist

1. David Sheff, "Playboy Interview: Steven Jobs," *Playboy*, February 1985, p. 52.

2. Ibid.

3. Peter Burrows, "Apple," *Business Week*, July 31, 2000, p. 106.

4. Sheff, p. 182.

5. Steven Levy, "Thinking Inside the Box," *Newsweek*, July 31, 2000, p. 57.

6. Owen W. Linzmayer, *Apple Confidential: The Real Story of Apple Computer, Inc.* (San Francisco: No Starch Press, 1999), p. 177.

7. Jeffrey S. Young, *Steve Jobs: The Journey Is the Reward* (Glenview, Ill.: Scott, Foresman and Co., 1988), p. 120.

Further Reading

Brashares, Ann. *Steve Jobs: Think Different.* Brookfield, Conn.: Twenty-First Century, 2001.

Gaines, Ann Graham. *Steve Jobs: Real-Life Reader Biography.* Bear, Del.: Mitchell Lane Publishers, 2000.

Linzmayer, Owen W. *Apple Confidential: The Real Story of Apple Computer, Inc.* San Francisco: No Starch Press, 1999.

Mayberry, Jodine. *Business Leaders Who Built Financial Empires.* Austin, Tex.: Raintree Steck-Vaughn, 1995.

Young, Jeffrey S. *Steve Jobs: The Journey Is the Reward.* Glenview, Ill.: Scott, Foresman and Co., 1988.

Internet Addresses

Apple Computer's official site, with a bio of Steve Jobs

<http://www.apple.com/pr/bios/jobs.html>

Smithsonian Institution excerpts from an Oral History Interview with Steve Jobs

<http://www.americanhistory.si.edu/csr/comphist/sj1.html>

Bio, photos, quotes, and video clips—including the famous 1984 Macintosh commercial

<http://www.geocities.com/franktau/History1.html>

Bio, timeline, quotes, articles, and lots of photos

<http://ei.cs.vt.edu/~history/Jobs.html>

"Steve Jobs at 44"

<http://www.time.com/time/magazine/articles/0,3266,32207,00.html>

Index

Page numbers for photographs are in **boldface** type.